BEYOND THE HORIZON

SMALL LANDSCAPE
APPLIQUÉ

VALERIE HEARDER

C&T PUBLISHING

© Copyright 1995 Valerie Hearder
Developmental Editor: Barbara Konzak-Kuhn
Technical Editor: Sally Lanzarotti
Illustrator: Micaela Carr
Cover Designer: Jill Berry, Artista Artworks, San Diego, CA
Book Designer: Riba Taylor, Sebastopol, CA

All photography by Terry James except for the following: *Vermont Hills, Shoreline, Reflections II, Winter Solitude, Birches, Moon Reflections, Natal Landscape, Ocean View, Grand Tetons, Cliff Walk, Kennebecasis River, Drakensberg, Larch Forest in the Snow,* and *Winter Fields, Sierras* courtesy of each artist; *Northumbrian Pentad* courtesy Merehurst Fairfax Publishing; *Prairie Sunlight* courtesy Darrell Kajati; *Gold Fall* courtesy Jeff Baird; author's photo courtesy Peter Barss.

Library of Congress Cataloging-in-Publication Data
Hearder, Valerie.
    Beyond the horizon, small landscape appliqué / by Valerie Hearder.
        p.   cm.
    ISBN 1-57120-001-0
    1. Appliqué. 2. Miniature craft. 3. Landscape in art.
I. Title.
TT779.H43   1995
746.44'50433'0228—dc20   95-18167
                                                               CIP

Fine Fuse is a trademark of Solor-Kist Corporation
Fray Check and Iron Off are trademarks of the Dritz Corporation
HeatnBond is a registered trademark of Therm O Web, Inc.
Metafil is a brand name of Sullivans
Plexiglas is a registered trademark of Rohn & Haas Company
Scotch 285 Artist's Tape is a registered trademark of the 3M Corporation
Scotchgard is a trademark of the 3M Corporation
Staedtler Mars Plastic Grand is a brand name of Nürnberg
Teflon is a registered trademark of E.I. duPont de Nemours & Company
Ultrasuede is a registered trademark of Springs Industries, Inc.
Wonder Under is a registered trademark of Freudenburg Nonwovens, Pellon Division

Published by C&T Publishing
P.O. Box 1456
Lafayette, California 94549

Printed in Hong Kong
10 9 8 7 6 5 4 3 2 1

I AM MOST GRATEFUL

to my husband Veryan Haysom who was always there to proofread, edit, and provide valuable insight. This book could not have been written without him. Thank you to Leitha and Roan, our children, for your support and love; my friends Pam Birdsall, Anna Davison, and Joan Johnson who read through aspects of the manuscript and provided thoughtful comments, caring, and support; Terry James for his fine eye and superb photographs; Randall Beck who has framed my work for 15 years; and to the good people at C&T Publishing—they were a pleasure to work with, especially my editor Barbara Konzak-Kuhn—for their guidance and support.

I am grateful to all the artists who contributed work for this book—both for consideration and inclusion. I could not have explored my subject as deeply as I have without the stimulating interaction with the women whom I have taught over the years—to you all, a heart-felt thank you.

With love to my husband Veryan Haysom

# INTRODUCTION

Fabric is so woven into women's lives that it is a natural medium with which to find our artistic voice. If you love fabric and want to express your creativity, this book is dedicated to you. It is my contribution to joyful self-expression in fabric. I want to share what I have learned about making miniature landscapes because the free-form landscape has long been my source of inspiration. A love of fabric combined with free-form landscape design can uncover and generate your creativity.

My goal is to inspire you to design and make a mat framed miniature fabric landscape using an approach that shows you a great deal about your innate sense of design—no matter what your medium or sewing skills. Some patterns are provided as a springboard, but I encourage you to quickly abandon them—they are subordinate to your own skill and design sense. Although many cannot imagine working without patterns, to do so is risking growth. Risk is necessary for creative growth. Following an intuitive approach to the fabric medium, without dependence on patterns, is a playful and rewarding way to tap your creativity. This approach, when used in small scale landscape designs, supports originality. Landscapes are beautiful, inspiring, and fascinating—the ideal form for spontaneous, pattern-free composition.

I encourage creativity with accessible techniques. Start by using the mat frame as a simple, powerful, design tool. With it you will learn to see, develop your design sense, and compose your landscape. Then by cutting into fabric, without using any patterns, you'll further realize your own ideas; it is an experience that liberates creativity. I believe passionately that we are all innately creative and that all creative gestures, no matter how small, are valid and vital. Many students have insisted they are the exception to my belief. I delight in seeing these women, after a one-day workshop, proudly hold their framed landscapes, their first creation without a pattern. This book offers you the same experience.

For twenty-five years fabric has been my guide as a self-taught artist and craftsperson. Sharing my love of appliqué fabric landscapes is the foundation for everything in this book. Love is the wellspring of creativity—let your love of fabric, sewing, and the Earth be the inspiration and joy in your landscapes.

Valerie Hearder

TABLE OF CONTENTS

PART 1
THE CREATIVE PROCESS

Miniature fabric landscapes are a coales-
cence of many elements: inspiration,
creativity, design, color, stitches, fabric,
patterns, learning to "see," and embellishment. All are interconnected and equally
important, but I always start with the
fabric—it is the connecting link for all the
elements of a landscape.

*"Every child
is an artist.
The problem
is how to remain
an artist
once he grows up."[1]*
—Pablo Picasso

Detail of *Horizons* by Kloof Village Quilters

chapter 1
FABRIC

Knowledge of cloth is key to designing fabric landscapes. Fabric is our medium. It serves as our inspiration for quilting, appliqué, and stitching. A love of sewing is integral to our love of cloth. We don't use pencils or paint—we use fabrics and stitches. We need to understand and respect the possibilities and limitations of our medium.

I grew up in South Africa, where the Asian and African markets hold a treasure of glowing silks, vibrant sarongs, and fine indigo geometric prints. My love of fabric began in earnest when I was sixteen, and I began making quilts when I was twenty-one. Quilting was a revelation for I finally had a way of expressing my ongoing love of fabric. When I later moved to Canada, my single bag was filled half with clothes and half with my beloved market fabrics. They helped sustain me through my first dark, subarctic winter in Yellowknife, North West Territories.

Leitha's Summer, 2" x 3¼", by Valerie Hearder

Artists develop a sensitivity to and a keen understanding of their materials. Our fabrics guide what we create and how we

---

Fabric generates the design.

---

create. It is the materials that give the clearest design cues. My approach to design is founded on this cornerstone—the principle is easily understood by anyone who loves fabric. My landscapes spring from my fabric palette. The larger and more varied your fabric collection the greater your ability to produce "fabric generated" designs. Fabric generated designs are those designs drawn by your mind's eye from your fabric collection.

Making landscapes in miniature frees you to experiment with fabric because only small quantities are used. The small scale of the projects increases your experience in designing with fabric. You can spend days and weeks designing a large wall hanging, or, in the same time, complete a dozen landscapes. As you make more landscapes, your sensitivity to your medium increases and you become adept at gathering and using fabrics that express landscapes. This in turn feeds your inspiration, design capabilities, and ability to be interpretive. The more you make landscapes the more you see landscape possibilities in fabric.

Crafting landscapes will change the way you view fabrics. I frequently hear the comments, "I started looking at my fabrics differently, I'm seeing landscapes every-where," or "I'm seeing the sky as fabric now." As you use a greater *variety* of fabrics, you can quickly build mastery and knowledge of the medium.

on harvest moon." You may find that some small floral prints can be busy and difficult to translate into a landscape. They can, however, be handled to work effectively. One way is to use enough to create a harmonious whole. If just one or two busy prints are used they tend to jump out, but if enough are used the eye moves more easily from one to the other.

Vermont Hills, 8" x 3", by Jo Diggs

Vermont Hills by Jo Diggs is a good example of prints working well.

Plaids and stripes must be carefully balanced in the landscape. While these strong directional prints may overpower a composition, when used in smaller amounts they can suggest furrowed fields or other landforms. Become aware of the contrast within a print. A white dot on a navy background may be too eye-catching and distracting. Large abstract prints, such as flowers and leaves, are effective when cut up and taken out of context. A shaded petal of a large rose becomes a hill. The pattern of the fabric suggests texture and this is what a fabric landscape artist seeks. Your eye will develop finesse as you play with these fabrics—trust your eye for what works in your composition.

Look for landscape possibilities in fabric.

Study the fabric choices pictured in the landscapes in this book and you will start seeing fabric as a source for landscapes. Some fabrics speak volumes about marsh-lands, a beach, or a forest glade. I am always on the lookout for large prints to cut up for sky, or perhaps a fabric that sings out "shine

Shoreline, 8" x 6", by Jo Diggs

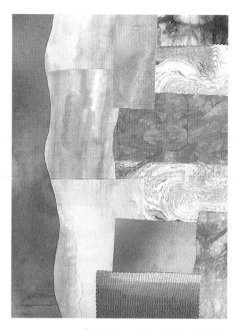

Swatches of hand-dyed fabric

Beyond the Commercial Scene

A current commercial trend is to print oceans, fields with little cows, clouds, and starry skies on fabrics. I find commercially printed "landscapes" lack creativity; I do not see much difference between paint-by-number and cutting out a pre-printed fabric landscape. (It is not exactly celebrating one's creativity.) Expand your creative interpretation of the commercial print. Use the prints effectively by cutting elements from the print, changing the context, or making a new composition. The commercial market will spoon feed us, but only if we allow it.

Designer Effects

The market is brimming with beautiful hand-dyed fabrics. Many quilters and surface designers dye or paint their own fabrics which gives them greater control over landscape effects. I don't dye fabrics because so many are readily available. I ask my silk painting friends to save their scraps for me. Hand-painted silk is a fabulous source of unusual designs because of the interesting organic forms and subtle shadings that make for wonderful natural-looking shapes.[*]

Swatches of commercial prints

* Review the Source List on page 79

Found Fabrics

Keep a completely open mind when gathering fabrics for landscapes. I mostly use "found" fabric. Found fabric is anything that has not been custom dyed or painted for a specific result. I am often asked if I dye or paint fabrics for landscapes. While I have tried my hand at both, I enjoy the challenge of finding just the right fabric. If you look in unusual places you may find treasures. Some of my best sunsets came from a shirt found at the Goodwill Store. Drapery shops are stimulating because they have such well-designed prints with wonderful textures. Crisp drapery cottons are twice as heavy as quilting cottons but still easy to hand sew. (Don't limit yourself because you think a fabric may be difficult to work with.) I enjoy shopping at dressmaker shops during Christmas and prom time for filmy organza, shot taffeta, and "dragonfly-wing" fabrics. You can also use treasured fragments of fabrics you've collected. Immortalize within a sunset a precious snippet of antique silk. Be serendipitous. Rummage in remnant bins. Experiment!

Indigo Mountain, 2¼" x 2⅜", by Valerie Hearder

Developing Your Material Collection

Miniature landscapes are a perfect format to try unusual materials. If you intend to frame a landscape, you can use fabrics that can't be washed, are of different weights, and are cut on the bias to generally expand the horizons of applying the fabric. Metallics are great for suns, moons, and reflections on the water. Netting and organza can be layered or frayed to diffuse a hill, give depth, or create mist rising from a lake, or clouds between the mountains. Moiré taffeta makes wonderful water. Even artificial silk flowers and leaves have potential. My favorite all around material is silk. Natural fibers are a supreme pleasure to needle. However, I have successfully hand appliquéd polyester (it is worth experimenting with, but it may need to be stabilized to give it enough weight for appliqué). Test sew a sample to explore its possibilities.

I categorize my landscape fabrics by placing them in clear boxes that I stored separately from the rest of my fabrics.

- ❍ sky and water (often interchangeable)
- ❍ land
- ❍ sun and moon
- ❍ leaves and bushes
- ❍ embellishments: lace, buttons, beads, braids, feathers, etc.

"The more you handle fabric, the more it tells you what to do."[2]
—Joan Schulze, quiltmaker

chapter 2
INSPIRATION

Inspiration is an elusive, almost magical, personal event. What inspires me may not inspire you. Why are some people inspired and others not? Is it possible to develop the ability to be inspired? The answers lie in understanding inspiration.

Inspiration is the infusing of ideas, images, or feelings into a person by a stimulus. This suggests there are two essential elements to inspiration: the presence of a stimulus and the ability to be infused and receptive.

An inspired person drinks in all life has to offer, and reflects that stimulation in her ideas, work, and feelings. You *can* develop this ability. It may require work and understanding, but the work is a pleasure. Feast your eyes, senses, and mind on interesting things. Collect and work with beautiful fabrics. Keep an open, positive attitude that allows new feelings and ideas to infuse you. If you believe you are uncreative and unimaginative, how can inspiration spark? Try affirmations like, "I am inspired and imaginative" and "My creativity grows every day." The power of such affirmations will enliven and support your creative expression.

A stimulus is both internal and external. There are many sources of internal stimulation: dreams, memory, intuition, and emotions. For me, inner knowing and inner seeking are keys to inspiration and creativity. This awareness develops my creative expressions in fabric. There are a myriad of external cues that may trigger inspiration: the environment, books, an experience, a visit to an exhibition. Seemingly external influences, like the environment, become internalized over time. The physical qualities of a scene or atmosphere may be inspirational because it resonates with memories and feelings that are already part of your soul. An iridescent silk taffeta may evoke the Northern Lights and inspire me to create a landscape on this theme. A gaudy Hawaiian fabric inspired *Tropical Dusk*. I cut away palm trees and surfers from the print, keeping the dramatic sunset sky and the distant mountains over the sea.

"It is
the creative
potential
itself
in human beings
that is
the image of God." [3]

—Mary Daly

Fiord Fantasy, 6" x 6", by Valerie Hearder

Environment as Inspiration

Your childhood has a significant impact on your perceptions of color, taste, and sound. I grew up in South Africa, and it remains a strong influence in my work,

---

Your environment influences your perception of color.

---

but years of living in Canada have cooled my palette. I noticed this when I returned to South Africa to teach. The fabrics I provided at workshops were not "hot" enough for tropical quilters—they wanted citrus yellows, shocking pinks, oranges, and golds. A student told me she needed brighter, stronger colors to compete with the constant presence of the intense, dazzling sun.

The colors in your environment affect your color choices. When I taught in New Brunswick, Canada, the quarter yard of orange usually shunned in my workshops was not enough—the influence of the area's tidal red mud flats and flaming sunsets ensured every scrap was used.

Your early environmental influences also affect your color usage and perception. When you are aware of this you can allow it full expression. Or you can make a conscious decision to select a different palette, one for which you do not have a natural affinity, and so discover new horizons.

"It's not a question of having good taste, but being able to taste what is around you." [4]

—M.C. Richards

Tropical Dusk, 5½" x 6", by Valerie Hearder

Photographs as Interpreters

It's important to remember when you work from a photograph that your medium is fabric. Photographs are useful in translating three-dimensional reality into two-dimensional lines, forms, and patterns. But fine details and effects so easily conveyed in a photograph are more difficult to achieve in fabric. I suggest using photographs for a starting point only. My purpose is to support your creativity and imagination, not encourage dependence on external sources.

I collect scrapbooks full of inspiring scenes, but I use them to make imaginary and abstract landscapes. In my workshops, I generally discourage participants from copying a photograph for their first landscape. It is daunting to choose a picture to interpret in fabric—one tries too hard to make an exact copy and then feels disappointed if the piece does not look exactly like the photograph. Doris Sagor made her first landscape in one of my workshops. Using three photographs of Mt. Rainier, Washington, Doris distilled their essence in her fabric interpretation without trying to make an exact copy. This successful piece was constructed with eight appliquéd shapes.

Mount Rainier, 6½" x 4½", by Doris Sagor

ChAPTER 3
CREATIVITY

Some people have a talent that is truly a gift, but we are all born creative beings. As a teacher I meet many people who believe they are an exception to the rule—not so! Self-doubt is the bane of creativity. We can lack talent and still express ourselves creatively. It is practicing creativity that develops talent.

Creativity is an intangible process woven from the fiber of our soul. It cannot be isolated and dissected, because it is not independent of the rest of our lives.

Practicing creativity develops your talent.

Creativity is a process, not a product. The creative process reflects our insight, growth, and openness. If our insight is clear our creativity flows. But insight is not all that needs attention. The inner voice of self-doubt needs to be silenced.

The Inner Critic

To some degree we are all subject to an "inner critic." That judgmental little voice in our head saying, "You're not talented. You can't design anything worthwhile. What a bad color choice." We try to fend off external criticism by being the first to judge our work. This negative inner critic blocks creativity.

Negative self-criticism is learned behavior, which can be "un-learned." To change the critical voice, identify it, what it is saying, and *who* is saying it. Often it is the voice of a parent or teacher. Be still. Listen. The chances are you will say, "What voice? I don't hear an inner voice." But by paying attention to your thoughts you will hear their put downs. Identify the words for

what they are—self-defeating negativity. Once you do, the negative inner critic is quickly disempowered. It's *your* head these words are running around in! Take responsibility to turn negative judgments into constructive evaluation and positive affirmation.

I empathize with feelings of doubt as there was a time when I believed I was not talented. Self-judgment inhibited me. Yet, I knew, intuitively, I was creative. By learning to hear my inner critic, silence it, and trust my creativity, I uncovered my talents.

"When we try to pick out anything by itself, we find it hitched to everything else in the universe."[5]
—John Muir

Foothills, 2" x 3¾", by Valerie Hearder

In her book *Ideas for Inspiration,* stitchery artist Pam Godderis suggests that most of us have not had many "places" where our creativity or uniqueness was rewarded and so we learned to mistrust our creativity. Pam suggests finding "safe places" to exercise and uncover our creativity. Places where:

❍ there is more than one right answer.

❍ how we do something, the process, is more important than the end product.

❍ we are not always told what to do and how to do it.

❍ we are not told we are wrong because we did not follow the rules exactly.

❍ we have fun.

❍ we ask, "What if . . ." and a variety of answers are permissible because we are using our imagination, our creativity.

My hope is that *Beyond the Horizon* will be all of these places for you.

> *"There is a vitality,*
> *a life-force,*
> *an energy,*
> *a quickening*
> *that is translated*
> *through you*
> *into action.*
> *And because*
> *there is only*
> *one of you*
> *in all of time,*
> *this expression*
> *is unique.*
> *And if you block it,*
> *it will never exist*
> *through any*
> *other medium*
> *and be lost.*
> *The world*
> *will not have it."*[6]
> —Martha Graham,
> dancer

Sun Journey, 4¾" x 7", by Valerie Hearder

chapter 4
LEARNING TO SEE

If you feel creativity and inspiration are elusive, learning to "see" is a concrete activity that feeds both. It is a way of seeing the world around you in artistic terms. Everyday, there are boundless opportunities to practice visual awareness. Like all activities, this awareness strengthens with use.

Learn to see by drawing. Suspending the mind and allowing the eye to lead the hand is a profound process of seeing. Betty Edwards, in her seminal book, *Drawing on the Right Side of the Brain,* pioneered an

---

Notice feelings—they sharpen your intuitive response to art.

---

approach to drawing based on the different way the left/right brain hemispheres work. (It is generally accepted that the left brain governs logical, structured, sequential thinking while the right brain governs intuition, feeling, and sensing.) Drawing is helpful to learning to see, but I also want to share other fun ways to learn to see and develop your creativity.

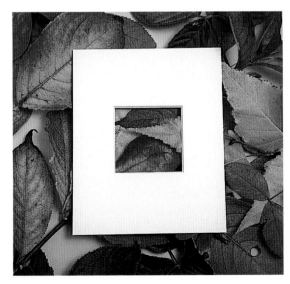

Isolate areas

Using the Viewfinder

By using a viewfinder to isolate an aspect of a subject, you change the context which allows you to view it in a fresh way. New meanings and possibilities are presented. Use the small viewfinder provided with this book for the following exercises.

Exercise 1. Move the viewfinder over objects in your living room. Isolate a corner of the carpet where it meets the floor. What shapes and textures do you see? Isolate patterns in the curtains, or objects on the table. Move the viewfinder until you find a pleasing composition. Then, with pencil and paper, roughly sketch out the composition. The sketching process develops hand-eye coordination. Don't worry about whether you can draw—this is for your eyes only.

Exercise 2. Hold the viewfinder a foot away and look through the mat window with one eye closed. Try moving the viewfinder different distances away and observe how the view of the shapes, lines, and compositions changes. Keep moving the viewfinder till you find an interesting composition. Pay attention to positive and negative shapes. Negative space is the space around objects and it is as important as the object you're viewing. Look at an object, and try shifting your focus to the negative space around and between the shape. Take the viewfinder outside and look at the landscape around you. The branches of a tree, leaf shapes, and flowers are particularly fascinating.

Exercise 3. Lay some fabrics randomly on the table. Observe the shapes, colors, and compositions as you move the viewfinder over them. Try to look for landscape forms. Next, lay the large frame included with this book over the fabrics. Keep shifting the

"Creative
or not creative—
no,
simply those
who look and see
and those
who only look."
—Unknown

fabrics to form interesting compositions. Add feathers, braids, and tassels for more interesting textures. Play!

Here are some habits worth cultivating to help sensitize your eye to design, develop your powers of observation, and feed your creativity.

Look for landscape forms.

Creative Clippings

Clip out pictures of anything that appeals to your eye, sense of humor, or for any reason. A visual feast is a stack of magazines to cut up all at once. When clipping, shut out critical voices, "This is sentimental, this is too abstract" that edit your choices. Remain neutral and open minded. You are building a personal visual vocabulary of images which, if gathered with an open mind, will stimulate the subconscious mind (your intuitive eye). It's important to trust your intuition. Allow your intuitive "eye" (right brain) to see the shading, positive and negative shapes, and contrast or focal point of the picture. Your right brain can see many lateral possibilities but it needs practice. A well-exercised right brain develops your ability to see and increases the sensitivity of your perception.

It is important to be nonjudgmental about your clippings. When you see a wonderful shoe, clip it (not necessarily because you'd wear it, but for its wonderful line and form). Appreciate it for all that it is. It may take years for an image to mesh with connecting ideas in your brain. For example, the appeal of an overstuffed orange leather chair may be baffling now, but when you look through your clippings over the years you may begin to see it connect with other seemingly disparate images. Together the clippings are clues to your way of seeing. Once you have gathered your file of images in a neutral way, you can glean information from it in an analytical way. Ask why something appealed to you. What subjects, themes, colors, or shapes keep cropping up? Look for connections and analyze the images that interest you.

Asking questions is an important road to developing powers of observation. When browsing through magazines, look at the less obvious for design principles. If you see a photo of a wonderful chocolate cake, ask, "What patterns and colors are in the icing? How is it presented? How is it breaking up the space?" If you are surprised that you clipped a photo of outrageous pink stilettos, ask, "What drew my attention to them? Was it their color, shape, or how they were photographed?" Look for a quality of line that suggests landscape. When you look at advertisements don't just see the "stack of towels" or "chocolate cake," try to identify landscape forms within them. As a landscape artist, you'll find landscapes are everywhere.

Books are one of the richest resources for design inspiration. Visit your library often. Borrow books on exotic subjects like Persian architecture or African adornment.

Exercise 4. Here is an ideal exercise for books and magazines which cannot be clipped for your file. Keep the smallest viewfinder provided in this book with you when browsing. Or make a bookmark out of an index card with a small viewfinder cut out of it. Run the viewfinder over pictures and isolate interesting areas. Try turning images upside down to see surprising new elements. These are aerobics for learning to see.

Visit Art Galleries

Attend gallery shows often. Don't limit yourself to art that always attracts you. Challenge your eye with works you do not normally like. Instead of dismissing them, ask, "Why don't I like this? Is the artist trying to bother me? Does the color disturb me? How does it make me *feel*?" This last question is particularly important. If you only respond intellectually, you are not using all your faculties fully or creatively. Feelings are crucial cues to self-awareness. Paying attention to feelings sharpens your intuitive responses to art and, indeed, all of life. If an artwork makes you feel queasy, question, "Why?" Your response reveals as much about yourself as what you are viewing. Visit galleries with friends and ask their opinions. Most importantly, suspend judgment, trust your feelings, and view with an open, questioning mind as your eyes "see" the artwork.

Observe Your Daily Landscape

Everyday life offers a boundless source of stimulating design elements. On a walk,

See the magic in the ordinary.

notice how the shadows of the houses intersect with the trees, how the sky is fragmented into negative shapes by a city skyline, and the form and line of a person sitting in a chair. (How does the body break up the chair's form? What spaces surround the body?) The kitchen offers pure visual delight. Slice a red cabbage in half to reveal the intricate pattern of folded leaves. Observe perfectly ordered seeds in a melon. See the magic in the ordinary.

Photography

I was a keen amateur photographer for a number of years (an interest that included being photographic editor of a folk lore magazine). I worked exclusively in black and white. Amateur photographers usually take better pictures in color because black and white demands a selective eye and restrictive approach. Those years of looking through a camera viewfinder were valuable training for my compositions within mat frames.

There are three essential elements in photography: shape, tone, and color. These are embellished with pattern, texture, and form. Shape more than any other element helps identify the subject of the photograph. When color is removed, one must pay more attention to shape and composition. Once you have played with the viewfinders in this book and begin to see in a nonjudgmental way, try the following exercise.

Exercise 5. Purchase three rolls of black and white film for your "point and shoot" camera. It helps if the camera has a lens with some telephoto or close-up abilities. Shoot all three rolls in an afternoon stroll. Photograph things that catch your eye: cracks in the sidewalk, roots of a tree, bicycle wheel spokes with interesting shadows. Your subject does not have to be identifiable and I encourage you to find abstract, interesting compositions. Use the camera's viewfinder as a tool (the goal is not beautiful photographs, but interesting ones). Set a tight time frame for your walk because you want to be spontaneous and shoot all the film. Later, study your photos but do not judge them. Simply select those which interest you. Now you get to play: turn them upside down, arrange them in groups, cut them up, and rearrange them again. Make a collage of elements and use a photocopier to make repeat patterns of compositions you like. Save the interesting compositions for your clipping file. Make notes on your designs and observations for future reference. This exercise is a great way to get design material.

"I truly believe that learning to see in the artist's mode of seeing is one of the roads that lead to the goal of greater creativity." [7]
—Betty Edwards, *Drawing on the Artist Within*

Record your ideas

Start a Design Journal

Buy a note book in which to write and sketch ideas, designs, or images. I have used various kinds of journals: a three-ring binder, a pocket-sized book with graph pages, a hard-covered, plain-paged drawing book, art sketch books. It does not matter what your journal looks like, as long as it works for you. Here are some suggestions:

○ Use it as a working record of what you are making. Record ideas, possibilities, and thoughts about your working process for future projects.

○ Record colors of the seasons, your garden, the shoreline—anything that takes your fancy. Use pencils, crayons, fabrics, threads, paints, and collage clippings to make color studies. These observations will form a valuable catalogue of color combinations.

○ Record quotes, paste clippings, and staple swatches of fabrics, threads, and materials.

○ Record embroidery samples and stitches showing different textures of grass, flowers, or shading.

○ Take your journal along when visiting galleries to record thoughts and to sketch ideas.

○ Record your dreams.

Feed and nourish your imagination with good magazines, art gallery visits, reading, and browsing. Develop active "seeing" habits. Your brain absorbs all images— likes and dislikes. When you start a new project, you'll have a tremendous gallery to draw upon for design support. Developing your powers of observation nourishes inspiration and creativity.

CHAPTER 5
COLOR

Our world is saturated with color. Color is so interwoven with design and expression that one can't avoid experiencing it. In this book I briefly discuss emotional and intuitive responses to color and provide some basic principles to get you started with your fabric landscapes.

The Emotions of Color

Color is closely linked to our feelings because it is a powerful presence in our lives. We talk about seeing life through "rose-tinted" glasses, being "blue," or "in the pink." In the same way the inner critic limits our creativity it also limits our responses to color. I believe there is no ugly color; it's a question of using a color in harmonious proportions and relationships. We have many prejudices about color. Many of us refuse to have certain colors in our house, let alone in our beloved fabric stashes. Some of us sniff at lime green and would not consider the rudeness of pure orange. Have you ever noticed that people use very little orange? It's one of those colors that seems to repel us—unless we are from New Brunswick! Our color preferences are natural, but we need a full and balanced spectrum in our lives. I have a friend who is very aware of the effect of color on emotions. She has a preference for the blue spectrum and realized that she had not one speck of orange in her house. She made a point of buying an orange mug so she could have a little orange in her life.

Why do we hold such strong feelings about certain colors? You may dislike pink because your mother dressed you in it while you longed for primary colors. Or you may have had unconscious, happy associations with certain colors that evoked a sense of well being. Whatever your experiences, your strongest feelings about a color are probably linked to an emotional event.

Reflections II, 8" x 5", by Jo Diggs

Here is a quick exercise to check your color emotions. Close your eyes and imagine a room that you feel is cheerful. Visualize the furnishings and walls. What colors do you see? Now visualize a room you feel is mysterious. How do the colors look? Compare your findings with someone else and see how your perceptions differ.

It is important to sensitize yourself to how colors effect your moods and feelings. There are no right or wrong feelings about color. Ask how a color makes you feel. List your color favorites and ask yourself why you like them. Examine why you don't like certain colors. If you have a negative association with a color, it's more constructive to resolve the reason why than to continue excluding it from your palette. Your ability to design is limited by your willingness to embrace certain colors.

Color in Nature

It seems impossible to find an ugly color combination in nature. Nature blends surprising colors in harmonious ways. Develop a habit of observing nature to gain a rich, broad knowledge of color. It's astounding how much color you can see in nature, even on a bleak winter's day.

When interpreting landscapes don't limit yourself to naturalistic colors although certain colors clearly symbolize seasons: cool blues and white for winter; yellows and pale greens for spring; deeper green for summer; and russet, gold, and browns for autumn. Try to make your mountains yellow or palm trees blue. The sky is not just blue—it's lavender and coral, black and peach.

Try these exercises and suggestions to develop color awareness.

Exercise 1. Gather thread, clippings of your favorite colors, or swatches of fabric. Paste them into your journal. Record any ideas or feelings associated with them. On a separate page, glue swatches or clippings of colors you *dislike*. Ask yourself why and jot down your response. You may find a new understanding of your likes and dislikes emerging.

Exercise 2. Use the viewfinder to isolate a small area of sand, lichen, or rocks—anywhere outdoors. Focus on a small area and see how many different colors there are. Record these in your journal with pencils, crayons, or threads. This will help develop your powers of observation and sensitivity to color.

Exercise 3. Soak in nature's purest color by hanging a lead crystal in a sunny window. The sun emits pure white light which splits into the seven rainbow colors when it shines through a crystal. It is color at its most intense. I hang antique lead crystal prisms in my windows and delight in the pools of clear, true color that shine into my home.

Color Principles

Many quilters and needle artists work intuitively with color. With practice you can develop confidence in your own intuitive approach. But it is helpful to understand some basic principles because color is an essential component of design. As you create fabric landscapes you will be drawn to the color of the materials first. How you use the color will affect your design; the two are integral. Contrast in color is basic. Color contrast embraces value, temperature, chromatic scale, and analogous colors.

Value refers to the difference in light and dark of a color. When a pure color is diluted with white it becomes a tint and when black is added it's a shade. This is how color value is changed. Graduating tints and shades in the fabrics can give a sense of

---

Expand your ability to design by embracing all colors.

---

depth in the landscape. An intense color can dominate a design so use it sparingly.

All colors have a *temperature*. Generally the warmest colors are in the red-orange spectrum and the coolest are in the blue-green. Warm colors advance and cool colors recede. As the warm colors in your landscape appear to come forward, they make the colors around them seem cooler.

"There is a logic of colors, and it is with this alone, and not with the logic of the brain, that the painter should conform."[9]

—Paul Cézanne

Detail of *Horizons* by Kloof Village Quilters

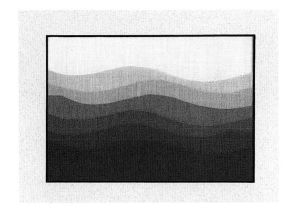

Value

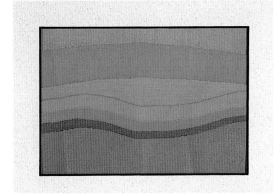

Temperature

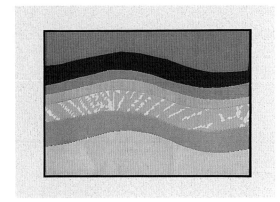

Monochromatic

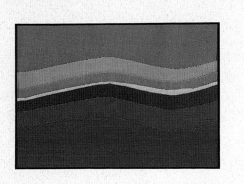

Analogous

A *monochromatic* scheme uses only one color but varies its value. Such color schemes blend well. They do not challenge the eye, but are harmonious, restful, and quiet. A *polychromatic* (poly means many) color scheme has many colors.

Analogous colors are close to each other on the color wheel. An analogous group could be blue-violet, blue, blue-green and green with a variety of values but all of a similar temperature. Analogous color schemes are restful and pleasing to the eye. A dash of the opposite temperature adds a visual spark.

These thumbnail principles are a very basic guideline for composing your landscape. *As with all rules, there are exceptions.* It is important to understand the rules but it is more important to be confident enough with color to trust your judgment. Then you can break rules. The small fabric landscape is a perfect format for experimenting. You have everything to gain from trying some wild, interesting colors. Train your eye to see how colors can make your landscape look dull or how a touch of warm color sparks it up—this color is a "zinger" in quilting lingo. The key is to keep adding and subtracting color to your composition till you reach a rich and harmonious whole. It is important to play as much as possible—to flex your color responses—so that you develop a keen sensitivity to its application in your work.

Chapter 6
Design Principles

Design seems to be a word that intimidates, yet we unconsciously observe and practice design in our daily lives. Everyday acts offer many opportunities to understand design: we arrange our "treasurers" in interesting ways, plant gardens, walk in the woods, and browse through books. Serving food is an example of a daily design act. We can slop the food on the plate or arrange it with attention to color, proportion, and form; gourmet magazines define food presentation as an art form. The key is to bring design activities from the unconscious to the attentive mind.

Understanding the fundamental principles of design will assist you in making small fabric landscapes.

Rhythm

Rhythm in design is the repetition of a shape, color, or line. When a shape is repeated in a composition, it develops rhythm and pattern, and this creates visual cohesion and unity. Our eye unconsciously seeks patterns and repeated shapes. Quilters create rhythm by repeating a patchwork block many times within a quilt. There is a natural rhythm and pattern in landscape features—waves of grass, wind-rippled sand, mountain shapes that echo each other into the distance—that lends itself to interpretation in fabric. Rhythm and pattern are key to capturing and conveying landscapes in fabric.

I enjoy *Floral Landscape* by Nina Lawrence because it captures the feelings I have of Natal, South Africa. In the winter months, the colors of the rolling hills are the same soft beige and wheaten tones. This wall hanging beautifully illustrates rhythm and pattern. Nina uses hummocky hills in the foreground and clouds of the same shape (but turned upside down) with a double-scalloped edge. The clouds seem to recede into the piece. The eye is drawn into the landscape center by a tiny slash of "hot" color. The narrow fabric strips depicting the flat fields pull our eyes through the riot of neutral prints to focus on a setting sun and rising moon which are clearly the focal points of the landscape.

This design of *Floral Landscape* works because of the strong repetition of shape. The fabric colors are similar and the busy prints are balanced by quiet neutrals. The satin stitch used to machine appliqué the shapes adds further definition to design elements. Look for the principle of rhythm in all the landscapes in this book.

Floral Landscape, 27½" x 23½", by Nina Lawrence

Line

In art, one generally thinks of a "line" being made by pencil on paper to illustrate shapes. In fabric, we make lines with scissors and needle. Shapes cut from fabric have a quality of line—smooth, flowing, jagged, or angular. My landscapes tend to have a soft-flowing feeling to them; the lines are gentle, calm, and create a serene feeling. This is because horizontal lines create a peaceful feeling landscape. Smooth sweeping lines can make a hill appear closer. Jagged lines are visually interesting because they break up space; they make hills look more distant. If you want a dramatic, energetic landscape you should use more vertical, intersecting, diagonal lines. Pay attention to the quality of line expressed in your landscape.

Winter Solitude by Jean Hillis blends soft snowy forms and a gently billowing sky. The dark, diagonal lines of the trees against the verticals of the fence posts provide counterpoint in the landscape. It is a visually rich composition. Fine quilting stitches add to the texture and movement of the work.

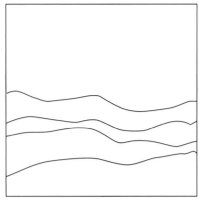

Horizontal lines are peaceful.

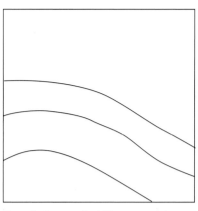

Smooth lines make hills appear closer.

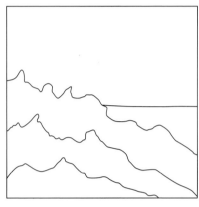

Jagged lines break up spaces.

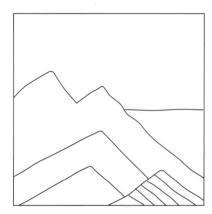

Diagonal lines are energetic.

Winter Solitude, 22" x 16", by Jean Hillis

Line is emphasized by the needle. A machine-stitched line can convey plowed fields or contours in a hill. Simple running stitches, or a dotted line of French knots, add line, depth, and texture to the landscape.

Contrast

Contrast is essential to design. Basic contrasts are light and dark, hot and cold, and flat and round. In *Floral Landscape* (page 24) there is little contrast. All the hills are round and neutral. The flat, hot fields, although very small, become part of the focal point because there is clear contrast within the design. A landscape without contrast risks becoming uninteresting or lifeless. But lack of contrast can also be used to an advantage. For a snowy landscape, try combining fabrics with low contrast for a soft ambiance. Some contrast is still required but it needs to be subtle. (Rely on your eye to discern contrast.) Look at your work through a piece of red Plexiglas® to reduce all color to a value scale. This will show which colors are too dark or light for the design.

Birches, 3½" x 7", by Jo Diggs

Moon Reflections, 8" x 3", by Jo Diggs

Jo Diggs, a premier fabric landscape artist, has a masterful eye for color balance and uses just the right fabric to suggest a scene. In *Birches,* she chose the fabric carefully to make the silver birches in the snow. She presents a study in contrast by using a full range of grays between pure white and black. Jo's *Moon Reflections* shows dark landforms emphasized by the strong contrast of the small, intensely silver moon.

Negative Space

It is a revelation to become aware of spaces *around* things, as we found in the viewfinder exercises (page 17). If you look at a tree, which is a positive shape, notice the spaces around and in between the branches. This is negative space. If you train your eye to see negative space, you will develop sensitivity to line and shape. By cutting jagged mountain shapes for a landscape, you can create interesting negative space behind the mountains. Try to keep negative spaces interesting when cutting out landscape shapes. Look at the landscapes in this book to learn more about using negative space. Look particularly at the sky areas. Is a sky neatly sliced by a smooth, distant horizon? Or do the mountains cut a jagged swath across it? The sky is negative space defined by the straight edges of the mat frame and the horizon.

Look for the negative space.

Texture

Fabric is inextricably linked with texture. We can easily visualize a slick, shiny satin, or the rough, raw earthiness of burlap, but when making fabric landscapes, texture is limited only to what will lie flat enough to "read" as landscape. Use only the appropriate textures for the scale of the landscape. Fake fur, wide-wale corduroy, and woolly tweed are tricky to use since the texture easily overpowers a small composition. Be aware of the feeling and atmosphere the texture evokes. Be willing to experiment. Try using frayed cotton and silk for water grasses. Unravel a coarse textured fabric, like bouclé, and stitch it onto a hilltop, or use part of it for a tree.

Prue Dobinson built an exquisite texture in *Northumbrian Pentad.* Sheer georgette, silk, and cheesecloth were smocked, pleated, frayed, and ruched into landforms and then appliquéd onto a background fabric. The frayed georgette gives a soft grassy effect and diffuses the edges of the shapes, adding depth and dimension to the work. The full piece is shown on page 77 in Chapter 13: Expanding Horizons.

Detail of *Northumbrian Pentad* by Prue Dobinson

Hooked Landscape, 8" x 6¾", by Valerie Hearder

For *Hooked Landscape* I formed a hill by hooking dyed raw wool through a loosely woven silk backing. I then built the surrounding landscape using silks and cottons. I enjoy using raw silk because it is available in many weights. Embroidery stitches, beading, and braids also add exciting textures to the composition. Here I added thickly stitched French knots, seed stitches, and beads to further enhance the texture.

Texture is closely linked to pattern. I rely on the printed pattern of the fabric to convey texture rather than using textured fabrics.

Depth

Overlapping is the basic method used to create an illusion of depth. (Both appliqué and collage are processes of overlapping.) To increase the sense of depth, try to vary the width of the layers. Layers that become wider in the foreground make the background seem distant.

Layered lines

Wide to narrow layers

Color is an important way to control depth. Warm colors advance and cool colors recede. I like the graduated effect of merging closely related values of one color together. Adding netting softens the color transition. If you use this technique and keep the shape of the hills flat and close together, you can create a sense of vastness and depth. A low, flat horizon and a vast sky within a horizontal frame can evoke the prairies or flat open land. By adding stitching lines, you can create a sense of hills and vales.

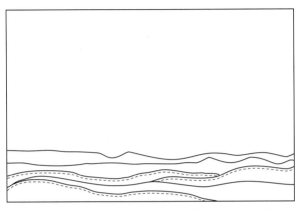

Flat, horizontal layers

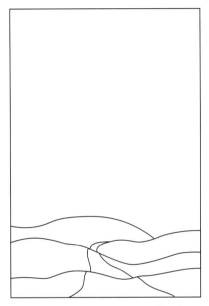

Roadway

Parallel lines that narrow as they recede into the landscape are a surefire way to create a sense of depth. Classic examples are a roadway converging on a point or a row of fence poles dwindling in height.

Another method of creating a sense of depth is to make clear, close-up details such as embroidered flowers, grasses, rocks, or bushes in the foreground. In *Solitude*, Laura Dekker clearly communicated depth by creating a close-up detail of grass from a frayed edge of fabric, and placing a tree in the middle distance. The sweep of a mountain peak in the background looks like a distant range.

These are my guidelines and suggestions. Ultimately, all design effects are manipulated by the composer. Trust your eye as to what you think works in your landscape.

Solitude, 7" x 4", by Laura Dekker

PART II
COMPOSING LANDSCAPES

When we learn about a new technique we almost always follow someone else's idea. This is a valid way to learn, but too often it is the only way we learn. We can become so dependent on patterns, instructions, and recipes for everything that we seldom make anything without them. Consequently, we begin to mistrust our ability to figure things out ourselves. An over-dependence on patterns dulls our naturally inventive mind and tethers us to what is known and safe. I believe patterns are a jumping-off point to learning a skill. Once that skill is mastered, you can then trust your abilities and create your own designs, patterns, or compositions. Liberation from slavishly following patterns frees your creative eye to design what pleases you. I get far more enjoyment in the life and inventiveness from a simple project of someone's imagination than from an elaborate detailed copy of a pattern. Ultimately your work will be more interesting if you design it yourself. The work will reflect the essence of you. Yes, there will be poor pieces, but that is part of growth. All designers make some less interesting pieces in their process of getting to the really successful ones.

I advocate and encourage making miniature landscapes without patterns. I use an approach which I call "cut and collage," essentially, designing by cutting shapes freehand without a sketch or pattern. The cut and collage approach to landscape design is dynamic. It is a synthesis of trusting intuition, playfulness, and skill development. I "dive in" and allow the landscape to evolve as I cut, collage, and change the shapes and proportions until they jell into a harmonious poem of color and form. I allow the patterns and colors of the fabrics to lead and inspire the design rather than relying on the set format of a pattern. Designing this way develops the intuitive right brain and offers many serendipitous possibilities in the process. It's also a lot of fun!

"You may miss opportunities the materials present if you adhere too rigidly to the plan."
—Unknown

(At left)
Summer Glory,
4½" x 6½",
by Valerie Hearder

chapter 7
cut & collage

My "cut and collage" approach involves cutting textured fabrics into landscape shapes and stitching or fusing them into place on a base fabric. There are several approaches to designing and composing a landscape: some of us like to map things out before starting, while others prefer to dive straight into the fabrics, cutting and collaging the design. I strongly encourage you to cut your fabrics free-form, trusting your eye and hand. Rely on the print and color of the fabrics to suggest a landscape. Cut and collage the fabrics, allowing the composition to change repeatedly, until the design is finished. I change fabrics and shapes many times until I find what works. The process is a dialogue with the fabric's color and form.

When I am in my landscape-making mode, I set aside a block of time—perhaps a week or so—to cut and collage landscape compositions. I find my design touch "warms up" as I go and, invariably, I discard the earlier compositions because I get better at designing as the week progresses. Once I'm in high gear I find that I am "seeing" and using the fabric more creatively and effectively. Themes begin to develop . . . summerscapes, night scenes, sunsets . . . I make several landscapes of each theme to fully explore the potential of the fabric and the composition. This process is highly gratifying. If a landscape will not "click," despite many cuts and collages, I am reassured by the knowledge that I have still gained valuable training in the process.

In this chapter we'll start making a landscape. I discuss each aspect of my cut and collage process and offer a hands-on "practice run" with demonstration photographs. In case you want to use a pattern before trying free-form cutting, I have added detailed pattern-making instructions. I've included landscape patterns for

Summer Glory and *Azalea Twilight*. Read the whole chapter before launching in—it takes many words to describe what is essentially a simple, uncomplicated process so don't get too bogged down in the description. What's important is playing with the fabric and using the text for guidance if necessary.

The Cut and Collage Process

These are the steps I follow when I cut and collage landscapes:

- ○ Gather materials and tools

- ○ Cut a muslin base as a guide for the landscape size

- ○ Make a viewfinder with the chosen size of the window opening

- ○ Start the process—working from the sky to the foreground

- ○ Establish the horizon line

- ○ Dialogue with the fabric (the fabric guides the design)

- ○ If desired, add dimension with batting

Gathering Materials and Tools

I like seeing all my fabrics for maximum design choice, so I start by stacking my wonderful fabrics and materials around me. They often end up overflowing onto the floor and neighboring shelves. As the design progresses, the stacks become frenzied tangles of sky and earth fabrics so I place the ironing board near the work table to press the fabrics as needed. I usually cut and collage about ten compositions during a week, and save the pleasure of hand appliquéing the designs for the quiet times in the evenings that follow.

Besides the assorted fabrics, you will need:

- ○ a mat frame (use the frame on the back cover of this book)
- ○ a 6"-long sharp scissors
- ○ fine ¾"-long appliqué pins
- ○ a muslin base or foundation fabric
- ○ *optional:* batting, fusible web, rotary cutter. For the pattern method, you'll need tracing paper, paper scissors, and a pencil.

The Landscape Foundation

The muslin base serves three functions: a size guide for cutting and placing your fabrics, a foundation for all the separate pieces of fabric to lie on, and a base to pin the composition to when finished.

Think of the muslin base as a blank canvas to fill with a colorful composition. The first step is to choose the approximate size of your landscape. In this example, the size is 4½" x 6½" (to fit the opening of the frame provided with this book). Cut the base fabric approximately 2" larger than the mat opening. Then cut the landform shapes an additional inch or so to extend over the muslin base. This leaves enough fabric to mount the finished landscape to the mat. The extra allowance will be trimmed when you finish composing. Also you'll have more possibilities when positioning your mat frame.

The Viewfinder

As was noted in Chapter 4: Learning to See, the viewfinder is a valuable design tool. For my cut and collage approach to making landscapes it is essential. The large viewfinder doubles as a mat frame. It is used at all steps of designing the landscape from sizing the piece, sizing the muslin base (if you are making a landscape to fit a mat opening), and composing, to finishing and presenting your piece.

Moonlight Bay, 2" x 2⅜", by Valerie Hearder

Once you start experimenting on your own, you can custom cut a paper viewfinder for designing landscapes of different sizes. As you compose the landscape, you may decide to make it bigger, smaller, or change it from vertical to horizontal, and then custom cut a mat frame to suit the colors and size.

Working from the Sky to the Foreground

I relish the challenge of making very tiny landscapes (the smallest is *Moonlight Bay*). Compared to larger landscapes, it is no more difficult to cut and sew a smaller design. And it takes fewer stitches! However, working in such a small space does require a delicate design touch and making careful fabric choices.

Choose the sky first. The sky is the background for the design and also sets the tone of the landscape. A somber sky with heavy clouds suggests a landscape with darker colors. A light blue fabric with tinges of pink and creamy streaks suggests a summer sunrise and lighter colors for the landscape.

Cut a piece of sky fabric and lay it across the top of the muslin foundation in a horizontal or vertical position. The sky

"Developing a piece of work is like working together with someone you like. You talk to them, they listen. Then you must listen when they talk! And so it is with your work. . . . Sometimes the work can surprise you a little. That's good. It means it has taught you something new."

—Jeanette Gilks, mixed-media artist

becomes the background fabric. Cut the strip wide enough so the sky can be either a deep or a thin line across the top and can also change position vertically or horizontally. This is where designing with the mat comes into play. Constantly evaluate the proportions of the sky and all aspects of the composition with the mat's window. If your landscape consists of mainly sky with a very small foreground of land, you can embellish the sky with layers of appliqué and fusible appliqué, or add stitchery to create interest. Avoid using the same sky color for your landforms. The eye will still read it as the sky and this creates confusion.

Establishing the Horizon

When we view a landscape we immediately seek the horizon. The horizon, where the land and sky meet, is an important focal point. For this reason, the water's edge at

---

When laying hills over a water horizon, keep them higher than the water—it looks more interesting and adds depth and perspective.

---

the horizon must be straight. If it slants, one's head tilts to compensate. I generally make any water level a straight line to clearly communicate "body of water" to the eye. Try using the top edge of the mat frame to help align the water's edge. When laying hills over a water horizon, keep the hills higher than the water. This creates interest and adds depth.

Fabric Guides the Design

Begin to cut and collage your landscape. Working the design from the background sky to the foreground (or top to bottom), start cutting the landscape shapes, keeping your scissors almost permanently in hand. The scissors becomes your brush, an extention of your hand, and the fabric your paint.

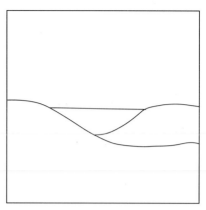

Hills below the water line

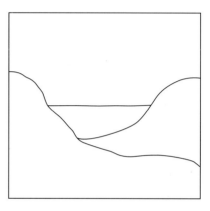

Hills above the water line

The first landform piece defines the distant horizon. If it's a high mountain, cut the piece and lay it over the sky. Now cut each successive piece free-form and lay down the pieces until you have reached the foreground of your design.

Throughout this process you will carefully review the evolving landscape by evaluating colors, textures, lines, forms, and how effectively they work together. You are working intuitively and synergistically with color, fabric, scissors, and your eye—all focused within the mat's 4½" x 6½" space. A large part of this process is trial and error or, more accurately, "playing." This is the fun part. There are guidelines for what will work, but no rules. Trust your eye. Pay close attention to the fabric and what it suggests. Let your intuitive responses to the fabric lead the evolving design.

While you are cutting and collaging, keep in mind the design principles discussed earlier, especially rhythm. Layer three or four fabrics together and cut them in the same shape. See how the pieces can be combined or layered in the composition. This is repetition and it adds cohesiveness to your composition; it tightens up the focus. Trust your eye to see if the shape needs to widen or narrow for best effect. A shape also can be flipped. Remember contrast? Your landscape, like a quilt, needs contrast.

Dimension with Batting

Batting helps create a three-dimensional effect. Incorporate the batting during the collage phase of the landscape. I suggest using batting only in the foreground. You may be tempted to put a little batting under the clouds to make them puffy, but, when viewing a miniature the eye reads the clouds as coming forward and this confuses the perspective. For effective clouds, try using reverse appliqué, fused appliqué, a running stitch, or netting.

If polyester batting is too thick for the look you want, split it to half its thickness. I use cotton batting because of its low loft and if I press my landscapes, the cotton batting doesn't flatten.

When you feel satisfied with the layout of your composition, iron and pin it thoroughly with enough pins to hold each piece securely. You are now ready to attach the landform pieces with hand or machine stitching.

The Cut and Collage Method

The following photo sequence demonstrates how I made *Summer Glory* (page 30) using my cut and collage method. You can get a feel for the cut and collage process by

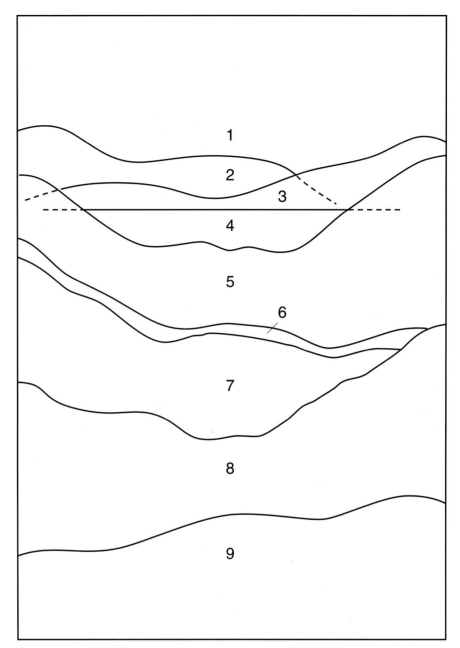

following the photographs. Do not try to copy every dip and curve of the shapes or your piece will develop a contrived tension. Allow your hand, scissors, and eye to copy the shapes in a free-flowing way that expresses your hand, not mine. You can follow my color choices or choose your own. The numbers on the pattern indicate the sequence of cutting the fabric pieces (from sky to foreground).

The beauty of this process is its simplicity. No complicated techniques or skills are required, just basic cutting and sewing. The results are elegant, and as infinite as the imagination. Once you have experienced the cut and collage process, you are ready to make your own landscape. If you feel you are not quite ready to cut freehand follow the instructions starting on page 39.

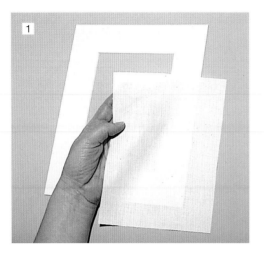

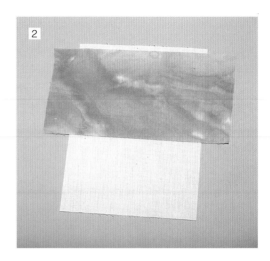

Note: Use the fabric colors shown only as a guide. I encourage you to choose your own fabric colors.

Step 1. Cut a 6½" x 8½" muslin base. This is about 1" larger all around than the 4½" x 6½" mat frame opening. The muslin piece is a reference for sizing the landscape; it is cut bigger as a reminder to cut the fabric shapes with an extra allowance to adhere to the mat. This landscape is being composed in a vertical position.

Step 2. Choose, cut, and lay down the fabric sky (pattern piece #1) across the top of the muslin base. The sky has been cut big enough to also fit the horizontal position of the mat. I iron the fabrics before I cut the shapes, because pressed fabric is easier to cut accurately.

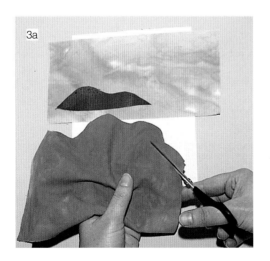

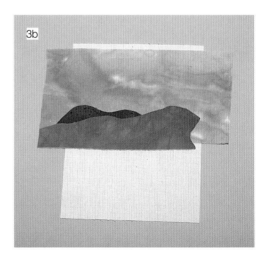

Steps 3a, b. Cut the background mountains (pattern pieces #2 and #3). I eye the proportions I want as I cut. These mountains form the horizon, and are laid over the sky.

I cut the top edge of the landscape shapes, without any extra seam allowance, exactly as I want the landscape to look. When the shapes are appliquéd, I turn the top edges under approximately ⅛" in sequence as I sew.

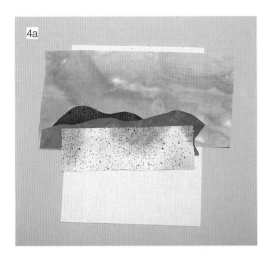

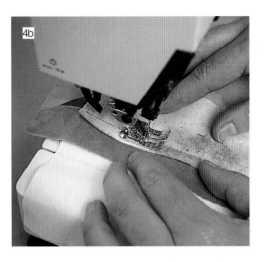

Steps 4a, b. Choose fabric for the lake (piece #4). Using a rotary cutter, cut a perfectly straight edge. Turn under a ¼" seam allowance and steam press the edge for a sharp crease.

Alternatively, this piece can be sewn down by machine, on the wrong side.

Note: The part of the shape in Step 3a that will be covered by piece #3 needs an extra inch or so of fabric as leeway. Pattern piece #3 has extra allowance that is covered by the lake as shown in Step 4a. Step 5b shows how the dark green fabric has been cut with a large allowance covered by the next layer. It is important to cut this extra fabric as it allows shapes to be shifted. The extra fabric can be trimmed away if you want to change the composition. Also, the extra allowance is an underlay that may be trimmed away to reduce bulk, if desired, when stitching the layers.

Steps 5a, b. Cut each successive piece, keeping the proportions that seem pleasing, or reworking them until you're satisfied. I like thin, outlining shapes in my landscapes. To achieve this I lay two pieces of fabric together (here the pale lavender and leafy green print) and cut them as one piece. Then I shift them slightly apart to add definition and a spark of color.

A nice aspect to this technique is that it creates a rhythm. You can cut three or four layers this way. I trust my eye to see if the outline shape needs to be wide or narrow for the best effect.

Steps 6a, b. Use the mat to evaluate and frame the landscape while composing. At every step I view the composition with the mat frame in both the horizontal and vertical positions.

It is surprising how much the orientation changes the composition.

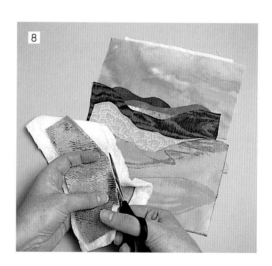

Step 7. Moving the mat frame 1" across the landscape can make a big difference to the composition. I keep moving the mat, covering and framing different aspects of the landscape, till I find the exact position that pleases me. Each time I shift the mat, I alter the composition so my eye is constantly evaluating the most pleasing placement.

Step 8. If some dimension is desired for the foreground, add a layer of cotton batting to the back of the last foreground piece. This step is optional.

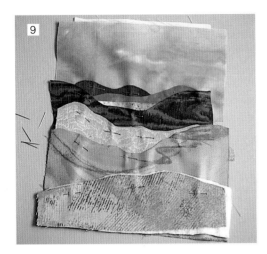

Step 9. When the composition is exactly how you want it, press with a steam iron. Use plenty of pins to anchor the piece. It is now ready to appliqué.

The sequence of photographs shows how to cut the fabric freely and allow serendipitous shapes to emerge. The pattern is provided only as a confidence boost and to give you the feel of the cut and collage process. If you want to follow the pattern on page 35 exactly, here are the directions. When you have created the design, try cutting a landscape freehand, following the demonstration photographs. You'll soon find you've no need of patterns and will relish the notion of cutting and collaging your landscapes. Note: All patterns are shown with an ⅛" seam allowance.

Pattern Instructions for *Summer Glory*

Step 1. Trace the numbered pattern (on page 35) onto tracing paper twice. One pattern lays over the fabric to check placement of each piece and the other is cut up, in sequence, as a template sheet for marking the cutting line on the fabric.

Step 2. Cut a 6½" x 8½" muslin base. This is roughly 1" bigger all around than the opening of the mat frame. Choose a fabric for the sky, which becomes the background fabric, and lay it over the muslin. Be sure to cut the sky to fit the horizontal width of the muslin foundation and keep it deep enough to fall below the horizon. You do not need a pattern to cut this piece.

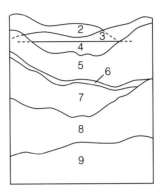

Step 3. Trim away the border of the template pattern sheet to the edge of the outside lines. Following the lines, cut away the #1 sky pattern piece.

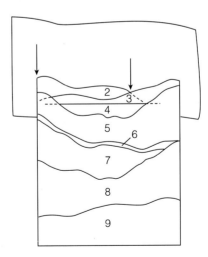

Step 4. Lay the template sheet down on the dark, plum-colored #2 fabric. With a pencil, draw on the fabric along the upper edge between the arrows of #2 pattern piece.

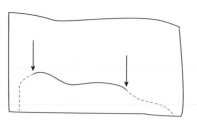

Lift the template sheet and mark the extended cutting lines on the fabric. The extended cutting line is shown as a dotted line on the pattern.

Note: It is necessary to add extra width and depth to each shape so that it extends beyond what is visible on the pattern piece. This extra fabric becomes an underlay that will be covered by the next layer. I usually allow about an inch extra but sometimes more is necessary. The side allowance is the margin needed to tape the landscape into the frame once the landscape is complete.

Cut out the #2 fabric along the pencil line and lay it over the sky. Any pencil line showing on the fabric will be turned under when it's appliquéd.

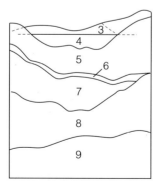

Step 5. Cut away the #2 pattern piece from the template sheet and discard. Trace the upper edge of piece #3 onto the blue-gray #3 fabric, marking in the extension cutting lines and allowing extra fabric for width and depth. Lay piece #3 on top of piece #2. Use the other pattern sheet to check placement of each fabric piece.

Step 6. Cut a straight-edged piece of fabric for the water (piece #4). Fold under a ¼" seam allowance and steam press it for a sharp edge. Lay the water over the background mountains. You do not need to trace from the pattern for this piece, but remember to allow extra fabric for width and depth, so the next pieces will cover the water piece adequately.

Step 7. Cut away pieces #3 and #4 along the upper edge of piece #5. Trace the upper edge of piece #5 onto the dark green fabric (remembering to add an extra 1" to each side and bottom). Cut and place the piece over the water.

Step 8. Cut away the #5 pattern piece along the upper edge of piece #6 and discard. Lay the lavender and leafy green fabrics (#6 and #7) together and cut them as one piece using #6 pattern's edge as a guide. Remember the extra allowance at each side and bottom. Shift pieces #6 and #7 slightly apart and lay them down over the dark green hill.

Step 9. Repeat the process of cutting the pattern away and tracing the cutting line for pieces #8 and #9.

Step 10. Lay the cut piece #9 fabric shape over the cotton batting and use it as a template to cut the batting. Cut the batting to fit exactly. Lay fabric and batting in place.

Step 11. Use the uncut tracing paper pattern to check the placement of all fabric pieces in the composition. Then lay your mat frame over it. Move the mat around until you like the placement. Now is the time to add an extra hill, cut the valley a little deeper, or shift a hill over a little. Play with the shapes. You can always put the shapes back the way they were using the uncut pattern as a guide, but this is your landscape to change and add to as you wish. Trim away any excess fabric from the sides but leave enough margin so the landscape can be taped into the mat (at least ¾"). The piece is now ready to appliqué.

Instructions for
Azalea Twilight

If you would like to try your hand at a more complex composition, here are the instructions and pattern for *Azalea Twilight* (also shown on the cover). The landscape was composed using the 4½" x 6½" frame provided with this book. You can choose to cut this landscape free form or you can make a pattern and follow the pattern instructions on page 39. If you choose to use the fusing technique, read Chapters 8 and 9.

Important: When cutting the pieces for the project, remember to add 1" extra to the sides and bottom edge of each piece. When working with multiple fused elements, wait to press the shapes in place until you are sure of the precise placement of every element (refer to Step 4 on page 54).

Step 1. Cut a 6½" x 8½" muslin base. For pieces #1-5 and the sun, add fusible web to the back of each fabric following Steps 1-3 on page 54. Choose a sky fabric that reflects a certain time of day. (I used tulle netting to add softness and depth, and anchored it down with a small touch of glue and the mountian's edges when they were fused into place.) Position the sky (piece #1) over the base.

Step 2. Cut the two circles for the sun. (I used a pink color and a shiny translucent fabric behind it.) Fuse the sun pieces together. Position the sun and the mountains (pieces #2, 3, and 4) over the sky. Position the water (piece #5) over the mountain pieces. Fuse the pieces in place.

Step 3. Cut and collage pieces #6-10 (refer to Steps 4-9 starting on page 37). (Leave a deep foreground on piece #10 to add the fused leaves and flower shapes.) Hand appliqué or machine stitch the pieces in place.

Step 4. The leaf and flower foreground was made up of three separate pieces. The pink flower was from a commercial print. The leaves were from South-African prints that were hand-dyed and individually painted using indigenous plants on the bank of a river.* Add fusible web to the back of each piece and trim around each shape.

Step 5. Fuse the foreground leaves and flowers. Trim away the excess fabric from the sides and tape the landscape into the mat, following the instructions on page 69. Sign and date your work, slip it into a frame, and it's ready for a special place on your wall.

Alternative method of cutting and composing: You can follow a sketch or draw the lines on each piece of fabric as the landscape evolves. Mark with a pencil or other tool and then cut along the line. Lay the fabric down following the same sequence as shown in the photographs. This is one step away from using your scissors as a pencil.

*Review the Source List on page 79

Azalea Twilight, 4½" x 6½", by Valerie Hearder

Help! I Don't Know Where to Start!

Remember, your starting point is the sky fabric—choose a fabric that suggests a sunrise or a sunset. If you don't know where to begin composing the landscape, just randomly choose a fabric to represent the most distant hills of the landscape. Tell yourself, "This is my starting point and I will work from here." Keep cutting and adding hills until you find elements that please you. Build on the pleasing elements. Start with a thread of an idea and start pulling in more and more threads until you have a strand to work with. Keep pulling in more thread—discarding what is not working—until you have enough strands woven together to form a strong basis for your landscape tapestry. What I love to see is someone cutting fabrics and re-arranging them again and again until a workable design is achieved. Do not stop at the first possibility—it is almost never well resolved. You need to work at color, scale, line and composition until a pleasing harmony is formed. A surprise element is likely to jump in as you keep trying out more and more options. Because you are not using a pattern, there are no boundaries for what you can try. This is a process that trains your eye to see and you are learning a lot about fabric, texture, and composition in the process. The design is open ended. See how you can use one piece in different ways to make it work. I often go through 10 or even 25 stages of rearranging, often adding and subtracting fabrics till I am satisfied. It is important to keep pushing to achieve a successful design. It is equally important knowing when "enough is enough." There is a delicate balance in knowing when to stop and when to keep going.

Often we want to make a landscape of a favorite place. Make a simple sketch if you like. You may find yourself trying to make the landscape look real, but keep your focus on the final design. A fabric landscape design is an interpretation not a copy of real life. Working from your imagination, you have poetic license to create whatever pleases your eye. Who says you can't have both the sun and the moon in your landscape? You are the creator and you have freedom to create whatever scene you want—abstract or realistic. If you find yourself working on a composition and it doesn't really look like a landscape but still pleases you, stick with your feelings of interest and enjoyment—allow the piece to express itself. If you don't like it, throw it out! They are only small pieces of fabric

South African Sunset, 4½" x 6½", by Sharon Falberg

and not much is wasted. Follow your heart along the path the fabric is leading you. If it does not look like a landscape, so what? See it through to its completion and then let your next project be a landscape. You are, after all, working in miniature and you can compose three in a day.

For me, *South African Sunset* (page 43) by Sharon Falberg could be a flower or a flaming sunset. She allows the fabric to lead the design. Often we are conditioned to be highly critical of our work. However, it's important to listen to how we feel about our work. In the process, we may uncover some pretty exciting design possibilities. The block detail of *Horizons* is from a quilt made in South Africa. The quilter chose a red-stained fabric for the water, but felt the color suggested a reflection from something above the water. Instead of the predicable sunset, the artist followed the fabric's lead and this sparkly, beaded volcano is the result of allowing fabric to suggest an idea and being playful enough to follow it through.

"Do not fear mistakes— there are none."[15]

—Miles Davis

Detail of *Horizons* by Kloof Village Quilters

Tips and Techniques

•If you are planning to hand appliqué your landscape, do not cut extra fabric for seam allowances. Cut it and lay it out exactly as you want it to look. Then as you begin to sew, turn each layer under a correspondingly equal amount (about an ⅛").

•Use the viewfinder provided with this book to find the most interesting areas in the fabric. The viewfinder will isolate textures, color, and pattern in the fabric and give you a sense of which fabrics will work most effectively in your landscape.

•Adding a small embroidered tree, animal, or other small scale element in mid-view adds depth of field and perspective. As you are composing the landscape, think ahead to what elements, such as trees or fence posts, you might add.

•You will hear "golden rules" such as "a piece should be broken up into thirds for harmonious proportions." Another rule is that the land that is close to you should be darker and then get lighter as it fades into the distance. This is what a scenic view looks like in real life. But these are guidelines and it is better to trust your eye to know what looks and feels right in your particular landscape. If a lighter color in the foreground and darker mountain in the background suits you, then let that be the overriding principle. Look at the landscape examples in this book and you will see light and dark distributed as is most effective for that particular landscape.

•I often have spent entire days collaging fabric to reach a workable design without success. The fabric snips may end up on the floor but my time is never wasted because I've learned to just play and use up fabric as I design. Being overly conservative with fabric will restrict your creative flow and possibilities.

•If the landscape will never be washed, worn, or subjected to the stresses usually sustained in a quilt or garment, you can break a few rules. You can cut your fabric on the bias, use narrower seam allowances, use fabrics that are not prewashed, or leave fused edges unfinished. You don't have to trim away the bulky layers from many layers of fabric as you appliqué the landscape. However, if you are going to apply a miniature landscape block to a garment, or a quilt, use these standard quilting construction guidelines: prewashed fabrics have ¼" seam turned under, cut away each underlying layer as you sew to reduce bulk (taking care with grain), and use stitches close together.

•Remember to regularly view your piece from a distance. A reducing glass or a pair of binoculars turned backwards is useful when viewing your work. A spy hole glass for a door works well and is available at hardware stores. Try using a smaller mat frame and see how that changes the landscape proportion. Conversely, try a bigger mat to see its effects on your composition.

CHAPTER 8

APPLIQUÉ STITCHERY

> "The 'artist brain' is reached through rhythm—through rhyme, not reason. Any regular, repetitive action primes the [creative] well. We've heard the stories of the Brontë sisters and poor Jane Austin, forced to hide their stories under their needlework. Needlework by definition regular and repetitive, both soothes and stimulates the artists within. Whole plots can be stitched up while we sew. As artists, we can very literally reap what we sew." [16]
>
> —Julia Cameron,
> The Artist's Way

When I have gathered a collection of landscapes to appliqué, my heart warms. I look forward to the quiet stillness of hand stitching. This process is my time to sit in peace and sew. As my hands carefully lace the cloth together, my mind moodles, meanders, and soars. The sewing machine certainly liberated a quilter's time but it didn't replace the tranquillity gained from handwork. Stitching draws me into an ancient female activity that connects me to my foremothers.

If you are not keen on hand sewing, I describe in Chapters 9 and 10 other quick and easy ways to stitch together the landscape layers. But I suggest reading through this chapter because it may help you re-think your ideas on hand sewing.

The Stitch as Line

The process of stitching creates a pleasing rhythm as the needle dips and slips in and out of the cloth. A rhythmic, stippled line indicating stitches is a beautiful testament to handwork. The stitches themselves become a pattern, an element of line, adding to the texture and design. There is no right or wrong way to appliqué—how you work depends on the effect you want. The stitches don't have to be invisible: a row of slanting stitches which outlines a hill creates a diffused edge that suggests grass blowing in the wind. A little running stitch along a raw, slightly frayed edge can add a soft, textured feel to your landscape. You can alternate the length of the stitches in order to create specific motion. Buttonhole or slanting stitches add wonderful texture. You can use a full range of creative stitches to get the look you want. If your stitching shows it doesn't read as sloppy workmanship, particularly when the stitches are formed with a conscious size and shape to show their intent in your design. Look at all the landscapes and study the use of stitches.

Ocean View, 8" x 3½", by Jo Diggs

Appliquéing with a Blind Stitch

Generally when I appliqué I use a blind stitch with a needle turning technique. Needle turning eliminates the need to baste under the seam allowance. I fold under the seam allowance with the end of the needle as I stitch to produce smooth edges.

The landform shapes are pinned down to the muslin base, exactly as I want the composition to look. I use short ¾" appliqué pins because they are easy to handle, they hold the fabric shapes firmly, and thread is less likely to tangle in the pins.

I do not pay attention to whether my stitches are going through to the muslin base or not. They do not have to go right through. While you sew, a few stitches will automatically go through the back but it is not necessary that they should.

Thread the needle with an 18" thread that matches the color of the fabric. I like to use fine size 12 sharps needles because the finer your needle, the finer your stitch. However, a size 10 is acceptable. When working on several landscapes, I thread about four or five needles with different colors to save threading the same needle every time.

A basic principle in appliqué is that whatever touches the background first gets sewn down first. Appliqué from the background to the foreground in exactly the same sequence that you laid out the composition. Do not start appliquéing the foreground first or the piece becomes bunched up and out of alignment.

Forming a Blind Stitch

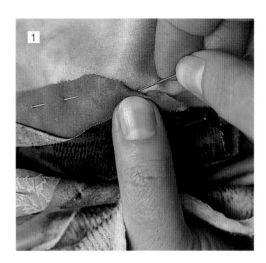

Step 1. Use your thumb to anchor down the shape to be stitched. With the tip of your needle, sweep and fold under about an ⅛" seam allowance, anchoring it with your thumb. "Finger press" the fold and keep it in place with your thumb. This is called the needle turning technique.

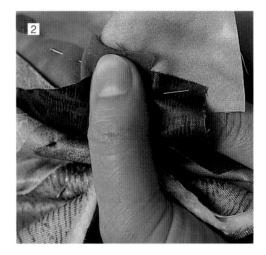

Step 2. Bring the needle up from behind directly into the seam fold of the fabric. The needle must go exactly into the fold and not into the surface of the appliqué shape—this is the key to a blind stitch. Pull the thread taut all the way to the knot. The knot is on the reverse side of the work.

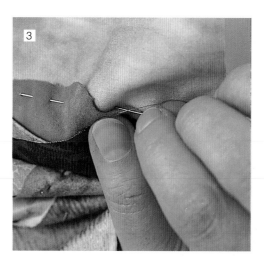

Step 3. Dip the needle straight down into the background fabric exactly where it came up (not ahead and not behind as this will make a slanted stitch). Where the thread comes through the fold of the top piece marks the spot for the needle to dip down into the background piece to form the next stitch.

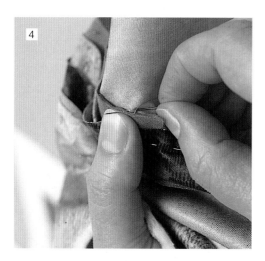

Step 4. Dip the needle into the background fabric and pick up ⅛" of the background fabric, coming up for the next stitch directly into the fold of the appliqué shape. The place in the seam fold, where the needle comes up, is the marker for where the needle will go back down in the background fabric to form the next stitch.

Step 5. When dipping the needle into the background fabric, tuck the needle slightly behind the appliqué shape. This adds to the hidden quality of the stitch. Remember to finger press as you form each stitch. Continue with this method to the end of the thread, leaving enough thread to finish off the last stitch.

Step 6. Finish by pushing the needle to the reverse side, and make a few double back stitches to end off on the wrong side. Stitching this way creates almost invisible stitches. An advantage of the blind stitch is that slight irregularities in the size and placement of the stitches are not obvious.

Machine Appliqué

Machine appliqué involves stitching shapes to a background. The satin stitch gives a pronounced outline to each shape. This may look too heavy but it also reinforces the design. Zigzag stitching with invisible thread gives a lighter look. For other unusual effects, experiment with the built-in decorative stitches in your machine. Wendy Hrabowsky used a narrow zigzag stitch for a softer line in *On the Beach*. Each piece is machine appliquéd and then machine quilted with a straight stitch. The felt fence posts were stitched down using a free-motion straight stitch.

Fabric Sketching

Laurie Swim developed a method of building landscapes called "fabric sketching" which she describes in her book *Quilting*. Laurie starts with a muslin base, cuts the pieces freehand leaving the edges raw, and lays them on a layer of batting. Once the landscape is composed, she adds layers of netting, securing it with straight pins, and bastes the composition thoroughly. She drops the feed dogs on the machine and "draws" lines with a straight stitch, making sure each piece is caught under the netting. (If your machine's dogs don't drop, tape a piece of cardpaper over them.) Once the pieces are stitched down, she trims away the areas of netting where there should be clearer color, leaving the netting in areas for softer, muted tones. Once this is complete, she decides where to add more stitching and embellishments.

On the Beach, 12" x 10", by Wendy Hrabowsky

Grand Tetons, 25" x 15", by Laurie Swim

Using a simple and effective approach, Margie Garratt has both appliquéd and embellished her landscape in one step. She cut the landscape shapes and laid them down leaving the edges raw. The foreground hill has loose snippets of fabric for dimension and texture. The machine stitched lines create contours while simultaneously tacking the shapes in place.

Cliff Walk, 7" x 5½", by Margie Garratt

Hand Appliqué Tips and Techniques

○ Curves cut on the bias swoop under easily and won't need to be clipped or notched because the curves are not steep. As you sew, keep needle turning under the little peaks and pokes that tend to stick out as the stitches are formed. A smooth edge is desirable.

○ Very sharp, pointed mountain peaks may need to be mitered, and deeply curved valleys may need to be clipped or notched.

○ Because the landscape is tiny it will be sewn up fairly quickly. You can afford to put in your most beautiful or most creatively interesting stitches. Use whatever stitches you are comfortable with, just keep them well executed.

○ Do not appliqué all the way to the end of a piece if it is hidden under the next layer. Simply appliqué so enough of the background piece is stitched in place to be covered by the next layer on top.

○ Remember that a body of water is flat. The water fabric can be sewn down by machine, or iron a sharp crease on the top edge to hand appliqué down.

○ When I appliqué landscapes I seldom trim away the bulk under each layer. However, if the landscape is to be quilted by hand, or incorporated into a quilt or garment, then the extra layers of bulk need to be trimmed away. As each layer is stitched into place, lift it up and trim away the extra landscape layers beneath. It is advisable to press the layers as you stitch, and then trim when everything is crisp and in place.

○ After I complete the stitching, my preference is to press the landscape with a steam iron. This flattens out the appliquéd shapes creating a slick, smooth look. If you iron in an upward motion, the edge of each layer is pushed up slightly to hide your blind stitch even more. The conventional rule is to not iron appliqué, but I prefer to be guided by what looks right for the landscape. If you wish to have a more dimensional quality to your landscape, do not iron it.

chapter 9
fusible appliqué

Fusible appliqué, also known as bonded appliqué, is an effective technique and the perfect application for miniature landscapes. Fusing involves applying a thin layer of glue to the wrong side of a fabric and then "gluing" it to another fabric by using a hot iron. (Although gluing fabric is heresy in our quilting world of 12 stitches to the inch, perfect patchwork points, and invisible stitches, let's not overlook innovative techniques that can be used when appropriate.) Sometimes fusing a piece in a composition is the perfect solution. When the intent is clearly demonstrated, it supports the integrity of the design. If this is understood then *any* technique—frayed seams, dye-splattered fabric, large stitches, knots on the right side of the work—is acceptable. It is not bad workmanship, but creative use of a technique—poetic license if you will. Fusible appliqué is perfect for miniature landscapes because you can create details to fit the scale of the work.

I first felt guilty using fusible appliqué because I thought I was betraying fine craftsmanship. Oh but it was so liberating! The more I experimented, I realized that fusible appliqué gave me certain effects I couldn't otherwise get: dimension and depth, the addition of new elements to the fabric, stabilizing fibers, building up layers without bulk, and a slick, clean edge. I am now sold on fusing. It widens my horizons for obtaining subtle effects within my landscapes.

Dimension and Depth

When mountains are fused to the background, the fabric looks flat and therefore further away. This effect is heightened when the foreground elements are hand appliquéd because the appliqué creates a slight ridge. This gives a subtle, tactile dimension and depth—a sense of foreground and distance—which can be further enhanced by placing a layer of batting under the foremost hills. It is the same effect as a carved, raised relief. (Refer to the discussion on Depth in Chapter 6.) In *Serenity* the water, mountains, and sun are all fused to make them recede into the landscape background.

Serenity, 4½" x 7", by Valerie Hearder

Adding New Elements

Landscapes are enhanced by elements like clouds, birds, yachts, or a rising moon. Small details like these can be difficult to successfully hand appliqué. Yet when tiny, detailed shapes are fused into place, they almost always become part of the fabric to which they are fused. The moon looks like part of the sky with no visible stitches to give it a raised definition. On closer inspection, the technique is apparent and the viewer sees that the detail has been fused rather than printed onto the fabric.

Stabilizing Fabrics

Fusing stabilizes the fabric's fibers so if it's cut with a sharp scissors a clean, unfrayed edge is obtained. This effect allows you to use loosely woven fabrics or synthetics you wouldn't normally use. If you want to stabilize a flimsy piece of silk or other ultra fine fabric for hand appliqué, the fusible web gives it body and stops it from fraying. Remember fusible web bonds when ironed and any underlying seams or stitches may show through. Alternatively, when stabilizing flimsy fabrics for hand appliqué, use a piece of dressmaker's lightweight interfacing with fusible on one side only.

Layering without Bulk

Fusible appliqué effectively builds up layers without bulk. For example, to build up a richly layered sky, try cutting thin clouds that overlap. In *Mountain Rhythms* five fused layers are used to create the water, mountains, and sky. The foreground is hand appliquéd. It is easy to stitch through one layer of fused fabric. Two layers is harder to stitch and three is not worth attempting. Again, one applies the technique appropriately.

A Slick, Clean Edge

Fusible appliqué is an aesthetically pleasing solution if stitches would distract from a flat, slick look. By using fusible appliqué, you have the ability to add tricky little details. For example, the sails of little yachts on a lake could look like lumpy white blobs, unless you are an exceptionally fine stitcher. But a fused triangular sail will clearly remain the shape of a sail.

There are appropriate and inappropriate places to use fusible web and you do have to make design decisions about how and where to use it. Fusing is not an appropriate technique on top of a number of stitched layers. The stitched layers show through the fused element when it is pressed into place, creating ridges in your fused element. But if the technique supports the integrity and intent of the design then use it.

Moon Over the Mountains, 4¾" x 7", by Valerie Hearder

Here is a basic equipment list for using fusible web: (1) Teflon® pressing sheet, (2) fusible web, (3) hot iron (4) hot iron cleaner, (5) sharp scissors, (6) cotton fabric (to protect your ironing surface).

Fusible Web

There are several brands of fusible web that are readily available at sewing and quilting stores. HeatnBond® and Wonder Under® have a paper backing that's useful if you want to draw a shape on the paper backing once it's been fused to the front of the fabric. The paper also helps prevent the fusible web from sticking to your iron. However, the paper is only partly successful in this objective since it frequently shifts and separates from the fusible web. Consequently, I recommend using a Teflon pressing sheet with paper-backed fusible web. Fine Fuse™, which has no paper backing, is lightweight and better suited for most of my projects. But Fine Fuse cannot be used without a Teflon pressing sheet.

A Teflon pressing sheet is an essential tool if you want to save a lot of hours cleaning fusible melts off your iron's soleplate. It protects your iron, ironing board, and work. I have used two kinds of Teflon sheets. One is a semi-transparent white sheet that looks like plastic and comes in two grades: regular and professional. The heavier professional grade pressing sheet is twice as thick as the regular grade and will last over a few years of normal use. Another type, which I recommend, is a thin, tan-colored, fiberglass fabric coated with Teflon. It is the most durable and rip resistant.*

If there is one rule for fusible appliqué it's this: clean your pressing sheet each and every time you use it. The fusible web leaves a hard-to-see residue on the sheet. If you fail to clean your sheet, your next carefully composed piece could end up

*Review the Source List on page 79

with a patch of glue right in the middle of the sunset. Alternatively, your iron gets gunked up, again! When cleaning the pressing sheet, do not scratch off the fusible residue with your fingernail—you run the risk of damaging the sheet. Instead, use a little wad of fabric to simply wipe it clean. If you are not sure you are going to do much fusing, I suggest you purchase a small trial size of the regular weight. Once you are convinced of its usefulness, a half yard of the fiberglass or heavier professional grade will suit smaller projects. (I find a yard of pressing sheet most convenient for my general use.)

Mountain Rhythms, 4½" x 7½", by Valerie Hearder

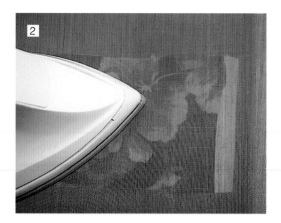

Fusing Guidelines

Step 1. Cut a piece of fabric a little larger than the finished size of the shape you want. Lay your piece of fabric, right side up, on one half of the pressing sheet. Cut the fusible web slightly larger than the fabric and place it under the wrong side of the fabric.

Step 2. Cover the fabric and fusible web with the other half of the pressing sheet—so it is sandwiched between two layers—and then iron the pressing sheet for about 5 seconds with a dry iron. Let cool for 3 seconds. Open the pressing sheet and peel off the fabric (which now has the fusible web attached). Wipe the pressing sheet clean with a small wad of fabric to remove every trace of the melted fusible. Be scrupulous!

Step 3. Draw the desired shape on the web side of the fabric, or cut the shape free-hand with a sharp scissors. Be sure to cut off the little "fringes" of web around the edges—these will stick to your iron.

Step 4. The trimmed piece is now ready to fuse to your landscape. Place the web-side down on the composition where you want it, and press lightly with a steam iron. You do not need to use the pressing sheet when the shape has been cut. When you fuse an element into your landscape, initially iron it with light pressure only to avoid a full strength bond. This will enable you to lift and reposition the piece a number of times until you are 100% sure of its placement. Then steam iron with a cotton setting to set the bond permanently.

Finishing the Edges

Fusing is ideal for machine appliqué. By fusing the shapes in place and machine appliquéing around the edges, the fabric won't slip while you sew.

Another way of finishing is to paint the edges with fabric paint. Generally I do not finish my edges. I like the look of a clean-cut smooth edge that "melts" into the background fabric. If I am concerned that the fused piece may fray, I use Fray Check™ to seal the edges.

If the fused elements in a quilt or garment will be subject to wear and stress, I recommend attaching the fused appliqué with machine stitching. Alternatively, a wall hanging won't receive the same stress and a framed landscape even less—here it is appropriate to leave fused edges unfinished. Use the appropriate level of engineering and technique where it's needed.

Tips and Techniques

•When you fold the pressing sheet in half (when putting the fabric and fusible web between the two layers), mark the inside with a permanent marker. I write the word "inside." This reminder ensures only one side of the pressing sheet is exposed to the fusible web and reduces your iron's "gunk-up" factor.

•Inevitably, no matter how careful you are, fusible will melt to your soleplate. I have found Iron Off™ the most effective because you don't have to wait for the iron to cool before cleaning.

•First fuse a piece of fabric that's larger than the required shape, before it's cut. You can't effectively cut out a tiny moon shape and then put fusible web on the back of it.

•Always test synthetic materials first to see what ironing temperature is needed. Metallic fabrics require a lower setting. Use a pressing sheet or pressing cloth to prevent curling and melting.

•If bubbles and wrinkles appear in the fused piece, it could mean that the iron was too hot or there was too much moisture. Wrinkles can often be ironed out. Again, if you have first pressed the appliqué lightly in place you can repair the problem by removing the piece, re-ironing it on the pressing sheet, and then re-applying it to the landscape.

•Use a fabric pressing cloth to avoid making your fabrics shiny.

•I drape clean muslin on my ironing board to make absolutely sure I have a clean surface to iron on. This saves a lot of wear on the ironing board cover, and muslin is cheaper to replace.

•Try gathering or pleating a piece of fabric to create the look of a plowed field. Secure by fusing a thin piece of dressmaker's interfacing to the back of the pleats.

PART III
SPECIALTY FABRICS & MATERIALS

Fabric is your inspiration—it is the raw material of your design. You don't want to limit yourself to cotton only. Quilters in particular are indoctrinated to consider nothing but 100% fine cotton because it is easy to control. Yes, often unusual, synthetic fabrics require special treatment, but that's half the fun and challenge! The framed landscape or wall hanging is not going to be washed, so you can add unusual materials without worry.

Creating miniature landscapes is a wonderful opportunity to incorporate unusual materials. Metallic, brocade, shot silk, polyester, lace, organza, suede leather and woolly tweed are all possibilities. *Drakensberg* by Pat Mackinlay (page 61) incorporates richly textured fabrics such as brocade, velvet, lamé, and tapestry. But less conventional materials offer exciting possibilities too: plastic, sequin waste, handmade paper, photographs, Ultra

suede®, feathers, buttons, shells, braids, and ribbons all of which could be fused, glued, or stitched into place. Explore unusual places for materials: Drop into a sports shop that sells fly tying materials. They offer exciting fluorescent threads and exotic feathers and their fishing gear containers are great for embellishment storage too!

chapter 10
specialty fabrics

Paper

Although paper seems like an avant garde material to incorporate into fabric arts, it is still fiber. Today we see wonderful quilts made with photographs and fabric—likewise, a collage of photos and paper fused in place makes an exciting landscape.

Sylvia Naylor's *Winter* reflects a cold, subtle landscape made with painted paper and fabric stitched with free-style machine embroidery. Sylvia hand made the paper from cream silk sponged with textile paints. The paper and fabric were then fused to a background mount of white rag paper. The distant paper hills in *Winter* are appliquéd by machine. Winter grass is indicated by hand-embroidered stitches, and glitter sparkles suggest glinting snow. Deidre Scherer used torn paper to create *Gold Fall.*

Netting

Netting, lace, organza, and loosely woven fabrics can be effectively used in landscapes. But these fabrics are so thin or so loosely woven that a fusible web may go right through them. Be sure to use a Teflon® pressing sheet when fusing them. Alternatively, you can stitch them into place. (A gauzy net can be stitched down with embroidery threads or invisible thread.) These subtle details make a big difference in a miniature landscape and your sensitivity to detail will develop with each one you make.

Netting is particularly effective when cut into several overlapping shapes to form clouds or trees. Netting creates soft, diffusive shapes that are difficult to obtain by other means. Netting and creative stitchery work beautifully together. In *Mystical Marshland* I used only two pieces of fabric: a brightly colored sky and a foreground fabric with fine gold stripes. I liked the frayed edge of the stripy piece so I machine stitched it down with reflective thread and left the fringe. I used eight layers of black, blue, and white netting to diffuse the sky. The black netting was particularly effective for the darker cloud shapes. I held the separate pieces of netting in place with a larger piece of fine tulle. Loose machine zigzag stitches are all that anchor the netting. After adding the netting, I felt the piece needed something more so I rummaged through my embellishment box and

Winter, 14" x 20", by Sylvia Naylor

found some peacock herl (used for fly-tying) that I glued to the foreground. The feathers look like reeds catching the last sun rays. They also add perspective, and as I view the piece I feel as if I am sitting among the reeds. This ethereal piece was really quite simple to make.

Fabric Effects

Beautiful effects abound in fabrics like taffeta, satins, and synthetics. Rayons also have particularly exciting prints. If you experiment a little, you will be rewarded with unusual effects in your landscape. Try using lightweight dressmaker's inter-facing to stabilize a flimsy fabric so it can be stitched easily. Most synthetics require a cool iron, in addition to a pressing cloth to protect the delicate synthetic material and to reduce shine.

Metallic fabrics like tissue lamé are effective and worth trying. I have successfully fused metallic, but it does tend to fray. When fused, add a little Fray Check™ to

Gold Fall, 6" x 6", by Deidre Scherer

the edge to keep it from unraveling. Put a drop of Fray Check on some paper and use a toothpick to spread it onto the edge of the fabric. Allow it to dry before fusing the shape in place. Use a cool iron and a pressing cloth or the metallics may melt.

Mystical Marshland, 7" x 4", by Valerie Hearder

chapter 11
EMBELLISHMENTS

You may feel your landscape needs nothing more than an elegant frame as the finishing touch. However, you may decide it is an unfinished canvas waiting for threads, beads, rubber stamps, fabric paint, or embroidery . . . the possibilities are endless. Embellishment is the final layer of your landscape, and if you have fused it together, you can add paint, beads, netting, or more fabric layers. Painted textures and details can be added before or after the composing and appliqué stages because fabric paints are soft enough to embroider over.

Embroidery

Pat Mackinlay used eclectic embellishments in her landscape *Drakensberg*. The small tassels, beads, buttons, lace motifs, folded fabric prairie points, antique buttons, and flower appliqués create a richly textured and varied landscape. Fly stitches and chain stitches outline the boldly-colored mountains. Pat strung the beads before stitching them in place and couched the yarn down with embroidery stitches. "Couching" is using a whip stitch to attach a heavy braid, ribbon, or yarn.

Little French knots suggest pebbles, meadow flowers, or snow fall. The versatile straight stitch, seed stitch, and stem stitch effectively convey beach grass, an embroidered fence rail, birds in a tree, or any motif you choose.

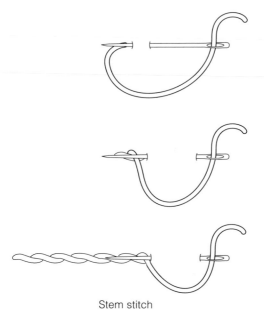

Stem stitch

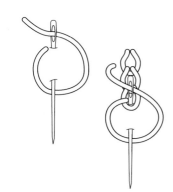

Chain stitch

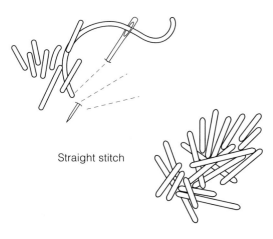

Straight stitch

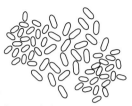

Seed stitch

Detail of *Larch Forest in the Snow* by Bettina Maylone

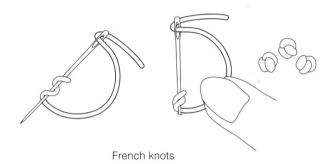

French knots

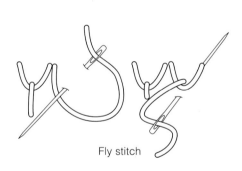

Fly stitch

Drakensberg, 13" x 13", by Pat Mackinlay

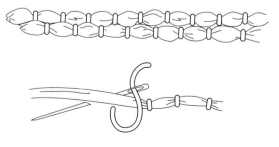

Couching stitch

Natal Landscape, 7" x 4", by Laura Dekker

A simple line of running stitches adds depth and perspective to a valley, or suggests a plowed field. Use embroidery floss for a lustrous quilting stitch. In addition to creating an element like a tree, whole hills and valleys can be textured or shaded with embroidery stitches as was done in *Winter Fields, Sierras* by Bettina Maylone. Use a variety of embroidery in your design to add depth and perspective. Notice how the peaceful clarity of Laura Dekker's landscape is enlivened with straight stitches and frayed edges.

Detail of *Winter Fields, Sierras*
by Bettina Maylone

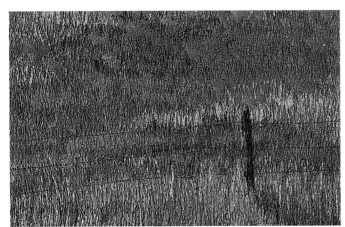

Detail of *Prairie Sunlight* by Martha Cole

Machine Embroidery

Machine embroidery ranges from simple quilting lines to complex thread painting. Fortunately, there is a recent explosion of extraordinary machine embroidery threads in the market: tinsel, reflective, variegated, dazzling metallic, glossy rayon, and thicker ribbon thread for couching down with a narrow zigzag stitch. The effects are so rich and exotic that it's really worth investing some time to play around with these threads. It is helpful to use a special needle such as a size 80 Metalfil needle. It has a larger eye and deeper groove and scarf to accommodate metallic threads. Shiny rayon or metallic thread adds to the texture of the fabric landscape as the light plays off the surface, accentuating its three-dimensional quality.

Martha Cole uses machine stitchery as if she's painting with thread. Martha's portrait is of prairie fields created with a straight stitch setting on the machine. Dottie Moore makes strong use of machine quilting to embellish and define her landscapes. More of Dottie and Martha's work is shown in the Expanding Horizons chapter.

Helen Brigham Opie embroiders the tracery of reeds and trees in *Kennebecasis River-Fall* (page 64) by using simple machine stitchery with a free-motion zigzag stitch and a darning foot.

Sea of Dreams, 23" x 23", by Dottie Moore

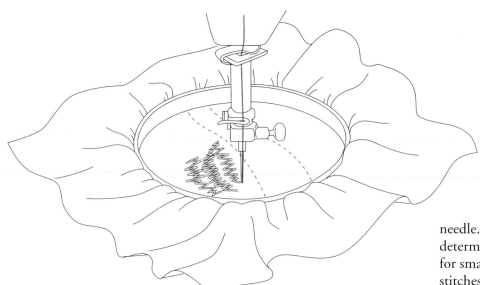

needle. How fast you move the hoop determines the length of the stitch—slow for small stitches, and fast for bigger stitches. Experimentation and doodling are required for you to understand the possibilities. Machines vary, so be sure to refer to your manual.

To try machine embroidery, secure the fabric tightly within an 8" hoop. Set the stitch length to "0" and drop the tension a little so the bobbin thread will not show on top. Or try invisible thread in the bobbin. Now remove the presser foot or attach a darning foot. Lower the presser bar to engage the tension and then disengage the feed-dogs. This enables you to move the hoop in any direction under the

Newer machines on the market have exciting built-in embroidery stitches which can be used to add motifs, textures, or floral patterns to your landscape. Take the time to play and experiment with these stitches and the effects possible on your machine. Once you start to play with metallic and variegated threads, you will be inspired to try more machine embellishment.

Kennebecasis River-Fall, 13⅜" x11½", by Helen Brigham Opie

Beading

A few tiny seed beads will add a sparkly, three-dimensional aspect to your landscape. Bugle beads, brass beads, and ethnic beads add atmosphere and focus. Beads are always eye-catching so be aware of how you want them to "read" in your landscape. They are very effective when clustered on strings and combined with textured embroidery stitches, netting, and metallic threads.

Detail of *Horizons* by Kloof Village Quilters

Stamping

Stamping is a quick, fun way to add images to your landscape, especially if you're not confident with your drawing skills.

To try out stamping, purchase some stamps and a pad from a rubber stamp shop or catalog. And did you know your local printer can easily make stamps from a clear line drawing? Be aware of copyrights, because you can't use someone's drawing or artwork without permission.

Make sure the stamp pad is well inked (without being overloaded). Stamp the image several times on paper first to make sure it is making clear impressions and then cut out the stamped paper image to check its placement in the landscape. Stamps register a clearer image on smooth fabrics such as a chintz or tightly woven cotton. I recommend using a darker color ink on a light fabric. Try various fabrics and see what works for you.

Use a thick newspaper as a base for stamping. If you are machine stitching the landscape, consider the stamp's placement before you sew. If you sew the landscape first, the stamp may not register a clear impression over seams or uneven fabric. However, fused fabric is flat and you can stamp directly onto it, as I did in *Tree Tracery*.

Try using permanent fabric markers or pencil crayons for shading, drawing in grass and trees, or toning down the contrast in a print if it stands out too much. Experiment, play, create, and enjoy!

Tree Tracery, 4½" x 4½", by Valerie Hearder

PART IV
PRESENTATION

Your landscape, composed and stitched with care and enjoyment, is the expression of your creativity and imagination. It deserves to be beautifully presented. Choosing a complimentary mat mount and frame is an important finishing touch. A key element of small scale landscapes is their preciousness. They invite close inspection and draw the viewer into the work. This is why the small details—the stitches, patterns, and textures of the materials and how they are matted and framed—are so important. The mat frame you choose is a clear border around your landscape; it defines the artwork.

(Above) *Down Home*, 47" x 26½", by Martha Cole;
(at left) *Tranquility*, 6" x 7", by Valerie Hearder

Once I'm finished composing a landscape, I choose a professionally cut mat. Unless you are experienced at cutting your own mats, I suggest you get your mat professionally cut. Although mat frames are fairly inexpensive, you need to take time to choose one that emphasizes your landscape, not overpowers it. A framer can help you choose one that supports your landscape. When selecting a mat, mainly concern yourself with the color and proportions.

Natal, 4" x 7", by Valerie Hearder

Choosing a Mat Frame

○ I have used both acid free and regular mats. An acid free mat board is the best choice; you need an acid-free board as it helps in the conservation of your landscape.

○ Cut the mat so it has a beveled edge rather than a straight edge. It is a subtle detail but miniatures require these subtleties. A beveled edge leads the eye into the landscape more than a straight-cut edge.

○ I like double-matted frames for my landscapes because they introduce a thin line of contrasting color which helps delineate the work. You can also choose a black-core mat board where the inner core of the board is black instead of white. It adds a dramatic, thin black line that can effectively enhance the design.

○ There are two mat types: ready-made or custom cut. Ready-made mats fit standard-sized frames. They are an inexpensive way to frame your landscape. The drawback is you may not find the right color or right inner opening for your landscape. However, a professional framer can cut the mat opening to the precise size of your landscape. You can then have a frame custom-made to fit the mat. Or you can have the framer cut the outer size to a standard frame size and use the custom mat in a standard frame (saving on framing costs).

○ Whatever approach you use, pay attention to the proportions of the landscape in relation to the mat. The mat should not be so small as to cramp the landscape or so big as to drown it.

○ Have the landscape with you when you choose the mat. Select the color by holding the design next to a window so you can compare colors in natural light. Artificial lights play havoc with color. Proper lighting is also a consideration for your work area. If you find yourself constantly running to a window to compare true color choices, you should consider installing full spectrum lights. They are a boon to any creative work and restful for the eyes.

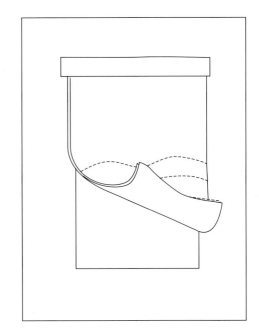

Mounting Instructions

I use this method for mounting landscapes in mat frames. First, lay the landscape face up on your table. Then position the mat frame over the landscape exactly where you want the edges to be. Note: water or sea horizons must be parallel to the top or bottom edge of the mat. If not, the horizon will tilt and become a distraction for the viewer.

Slip your hand under the landscape keeping the mat in position over it. Using both hands to hold everything in place, carefully flip the landscape and mat upside down onto the table. Do not let anything shift.

Tape the top of the landscape in place. Carefully flip it over, so it is face up, and check that everything is still in line. If not, remove the tape, reposition the landscape, and try again until it's straight.

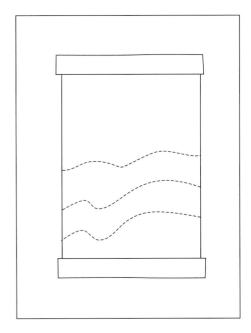

Once you are sure the landscape is straight, tape the top firmly onto the mat. Pull the fabric down slightly so it is taut, and then tape down the bottom edge.

Next, tape down one side and then tape the other while pulling the landscape taut. Pulling it tight eases out the wrinkles. Don't pull so tight that you put stress on the stitches or pull the landscape away from the tape.

With a burnishing tool—I use my scissors handle—rub the tape vigorously so that it adheres firmly to the mat.

A note on tape: the advantage of using tape is that it is not bulky. I find ¾" tape adequate for the job. I have used masking tape with some success but it can be unreliable. Over the years the glue dries out, causing the landscape to slip, and then wrinkles develop. I have found white Scotch 285 Artist's Tape® is strong and long lasting. But there are many suitable brands of white artist tapes (available at art supply stores), some of which are acid free.

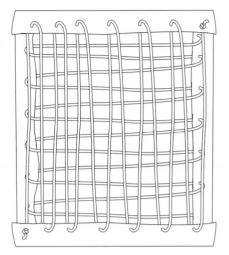

Pull the edges taut

Lacing Instructions

An alternative method for mounting landscapes is to stretch the landscape over a piece of acid-free mat board, and then carefully lace the edges to pull the landscape taut. Tape the landscape into the mat frame using white artist's tape. One disadvantage is that the bulk of the fabric may make it difficult to fit the landscape into a standard frame. This method of mounting the landscape is helpful for the larger designs that cannot be taped into the mat without wrinkling.

Autumn Glory,
5½" x 7",
by Valerie Hearder

Sign Your Work

We have a vast history of anonymous women's art, and so much is lost when work is unsigned. A significant depth of understanding is now being discovered about women's lives through quilt research. When a signed quilt is discovered, there is rejoicing because it enables researchers to trace the woman's life and learn more about her experiences.

Over the years I have watched many women sign their work in my workshops. It is fascinating to see the range of responses. Some sign with timid initials, some with a flourishing full name, some hide their names on the back, and some could not sign their names at all (perhaps symbolic of a lack of recognition in their daily lives). For most, though, it is the final exclamation mark to their work. Delight and pride are felt when a piece of work is signed. It proclaims the maker as an artist. Always sign and date your work, and use a graphite pencil because ink fades.

Frames

Some people don't like to see glass over fabric because it removes the fabric from the viewer and distracts from its tactile quality. However, this is a personal preference. I do put my pieces under glass because it keeps them dust and pollution free (helping to preserve the textiles). This is especially important when delicate materials, such as feathers or fragile silk, have been used. I prefer regular glass; I find non-glare glass obscures the image.

If you don't like the idea of fabric behind glass you could try using Scotchgard™ to protect the work from fingers and dust. There is an ecologically sound Scotchgard formula on the market.

I prefer simple metal or wood frames which are not too ornate or distracting. I have also frequently used a simple gallery mount of glass attached by four clips.

chapter 13
EXPANDING HORIZONS

Landscape quilts and wall hangings are appearing more frequently as people are drawn to the natural forms of our environment. The Green Quilts movement, founded by Susan Shie, spurred the production of wonderful landscape quilts as affirmations for a peaceful Earth. This movement encourages conscious thought of a healthy, pollution-free Earth. Hundreds of Green Quilts are being exhibited around the world resonating a message of a whole, healed planet. It is a significant contribution.

Many of the principles and techniques described in this book can be applied to designing and making larger wall hangings, quilts, or garments. This chapter shows how various artists have presented landscape themes. Once you feel comfortable making landscapes in miniature, you may want to experiment with larger ones as you develop your own style and expression.

My miniature landscapes have naturally evolved into larger wall hangings. I often start composing a wall hanging by making a small scale landscape as its heart. I expand the landscape into its surrounding borders. The landscape becomes an element of a larger, more abstract composition.

Solar Flare began as a small hand-appliquéd landscape made with the cut and collage method. I incorporated it into a larger landscape that extends the hills and sky. The landscape overflows the inner frame to suggest infinity. The cool greens of the landscape and blue of the sky emphasize intense, blazing flares. I fused the sun from a variety of fabrics, and then machine appliquéd it with glowing, fluorescent threads. The fields are machine quilted.

Solar Flare, 33" x 36",
by Valerie Hearder

"Pretend
you are dancing
or singing
a picture.
A worker
or painter
should enjoy
his work,
else the observer
will not enjoy it.
It is not good
to wear lace
that was
a drudgery
for someone
to make.
The lace,
as well as
the picture,
should be made
in joy.
All real
works of art
look as though
they were done
in joy." [17]

—Robert Henri,
The Art Spirit

Tropic of Capricorn evolved in a similar fashion. I wanted to convey a feeling of a verdant, tropical land with a blazing hot sun. I developed the central landscape panel first. The lush leaves were cut from many different fabrics and fused into place, as were the purple anemones. The inner landscape overflows into the border, integrating the two elements of the composition. Geometric shapes are a counterpoint to the soft landscape. I like using unusual shapes to add a lyrical flow. *Tropic of Capricorn* incorporates metallic, cotton, polyester, silk, and taffeta fabrics. Taffeta, while difficult to work with, gives rich depth to the border. This piece was designed using the cut and collage method.

Tropic of Capricorn, 28" x 36", by Valerie Hearder

In *Homelands* I first made the subtle, bleached landscape and then linked it with its strong surrounding border. I included African indigo cotton and brass beads. There is an ethereal, pale triangle of organza in the sky which represents ancestral spirits. I didn't quilt *Tropic of Capricorn* or *Homelands* because I wanted a flat, slick look.

Dottie Moore uses inner frames in her wall hangings, suggesting windows that draw the viewer into the landscape. The landscapes are serene and dreamlike. The intense machine quilting gives them an almost sculptured feel. Dottie describes her pieces as developing a whole conversation in a single image. Careful use of foreground elements like trees, roots, and flowers allows one to feel close to the scene yet still view the plane as distant—an ambiguous approach which creates a wonderful sense of depth.

Dottie cuts fabrics freehand and doesn't mind making mistakes. She throws the fabric away and starts over. Dottie uses cotton and cotton-blends augmented with a diluted wash of fabric paint. Once the design is complete she sandwiches the top, batting, and backing with pins and begins machine quilting. The major lines are sewn first; then she fills small areas with textured stitching, creating "auras" of colorful lines around trees and flowers. Using straight stitch, zigzag, and darning feet, she machine quilts using up to fifty spools of thread in one quilt. Dottie refers to her machine as a "motorized needle." Finally, small elements such as leaves, buds, and flowers are hand embroidered using simple French knots and lazy daisy stitches. One of Dottie's landscapes is in the White House.

Homelands, 20" x 32", by Valerie Hearder

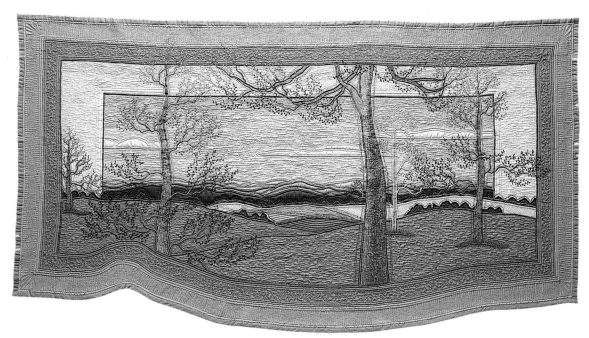

Meditation,
72" x 37",
by Dottie Moore

Horizons, 6½' x 6½', by Kloof Village Quilters

The miniature landscapes in *Horizons* are autonomous works by different quilters. Each block is framed in an off-kilter Log Cabin border. Repetition ties the landscapes together to make a strikingly successful quilt. (The Kloof Village Quilters credit the author's workshops for their inspiration.)

Landscapes: Our Heritage, 6½' x 4½', by Kloof Village Quilters

The next quilt from this talented group is *Landscapes: Our Heritage*, which won five top ribbons at the 1994 National Quilt Festival in Cape Town, South Africa. *Landscapes: Our Heritage* is a more complex composition. Each landscape is composed to accurately portray a special scene. A unifying, painted background landscape links each separate scene to the whole. But some of the individual landscapes overflow their frames to link with the larger landscape. Water, earth, and sky are balanced throughout in a harmonious blend of elements. It is a wonderfully hopeful and symbolic quilt made in the year that South Africa held its first free elections.

Elysian Hills, 25" x 32",
by Deidre Scherer

Elysian Hills by Deidre Scherer is an actual Vermont view in fall foliage. First Deidre drew the scene with pencil and crayons and then translated the look and feel into fabric. She machine stitched a portrait of the beautiful hills, fields, and stately trees.

Martha Cole mottles all her fabrics using light washes of acrylic paint. She transfers her drawings to the fabric, and then cuts and places the pieces onto cotton backing to machine appliqué. Martha uses very few pieces of fabric. There is only one hill in *Prairie Sunlight*. To create depth and give the effect of light catching the prairie grasses, she uses the machine as an electric paintbrush to build shading with a free-motion straight stitch. The strong geometric patchwork is a wonderful counterpoint to a realistic rendering of the landscape. Once the piece is stitched, Martha adds machine quilting to the sky. The quilting on top of the machine stitchery adds layered richness to the texture. One can almost feel the expansive sky and land in the evocative landscapes of Martha Cole. The feeling of light and ripply wheat gives her wall hanging a life force. Her home in Saskatchewan, in the heart of the Canadian prairies, is an endless source of inspiration for Martha.

Prairie Sunlight, 32" x 24",
by Martha Cole

Bettina Maylone used hand stitching to mimic the Sierra grasslands. Hand embroidery and appliqué provide Bettina with a richness in embellishment she has not been able to duplicate in paint or other media. For Bettina the process of making fabric images of the Earth is a way of honoring and prolonging her experiences in the natural world. She uses a photograph or drawing, which she willingly changes in the design process, as a starting point. Using the cut and collage approach, Bettina begins at the furthest point and works towards the foreground. Practicing what she calls "substance abuse," she will wrinkle, singe, tear, unravel, stain, or otherwise tamper with the materials. Each element is an exploration of an idea and the materials that support it. Bettina uses acrylic paint or lightfast Staedtler

Winter Field, Sierras, 30" x 24", by Bettina Maylone

inks to shade areas of cloth. *Winter Field, Sierras* is appliquéed and embroidered satin, silk, cotton, linen, upholstery fabric, netting, and leather. Bettina relishes manipulating her materials to get the effects she wants. Her spirit is reflected in her work.

Prue Dobinson pushes the boundaries of fabric manipulation to get magical effects. In *Northumbrian Pentad*, Prue mounted the landscape on a board in five sections. Large foreground stitches enhance the sense of depth. Prue, like Bettina, has fully explored and used her materials to get the effects she wants. The result is a richly textured landscape and a beautiful, lively surface that invites the eye to explore.

Detail of *Northumbrian Pentad*, 24" x 36", by Prue Dobinson

CONCLUSION

This book is a synthesis of my learning and growth. My learning embraces the women who taught me in my childhood, adult life, and in my classes.

I first learned to sew from my mother and a wonderfully strict domestic science teacher, who had also taught my mother. When I was ten, Miss Moe taught me two things: "you can't use a dagger to sew with—a fine needle gives a fine stitch" and "the fabric will go where you want it to go." I simply had no excuses in her class! I think of these as Miss Moe's maxims and when I'm wrestling with a tricky design, I recall her words and they always help.

My hope is that my book has passed on the best I have to offer. I encourage you to explore, experiment, push the horizons of these ideas and techniques, and adopt what works for you in your fabric expressions. I hope *Beyond the Horizon* will inspire you, support your creativity, and make you want to hurry to your fabrics and threads. When you get there, I can do no better than Miss Moe and say, "Make them go where you want them to go!"

Moonrise, 48" x 36", by Valerie Hearder

Source List

Fabrics

Bizarre Bazaar, 8553 Loughery Rd., Box 356, Indiana, WA, 98342 USA (South African hand-dyed fabrics; write for information)

The Cotton Patch, 1025 Brown Ave., Lafayette, CA 94549 USA (Large selection of contemporary and solid cotton fabrics. Call for catalog. 800-835-4418)

Judi's Hand-Dyed Fabrics, 1518 Slocan St., Nelson, BC, V1L 1E9 Canada (catalog)

Mickey Lawler's Skydyes, 83 Richmond Lane, W. Hartford, CT, 06117 USA (hand-dyed sky and land fabrics)

Shades Inc., The Nunn Complex, Studio O, 585 Cobb Parkway, S. Marietta, GA, 30062 USA (hand-dyed sky fabric)

The Uncommon Thread, P.O. Box 335, Lincoln, MA, 01773 USA (South African hand-dyed and silk-screen designer fabric; catalog)

Notions

A Great Notion, Sewing Supply Ltd., 13847 17A Ave., White Rock, BC, V4A 7H4 Canada (Teflon® pressing sheets and hard to find supplies; catalog)

Aardvark Adventures, Box 2449, Livermore, CA, 94550 USA (embellishments, threads, needles, books; newsletter/catalog)

Angelsea FaerieTale Ornament, P.O. Box 4586, Stockton, CA, 95204 USA (ribbons, silk-ribbon embroidery, threads, braids, tassels, fabric; catalog)

Thread Shed, P.O. Box 898, Horse Shoe, NC, 28742 USA (metallic threads, bulk spools, machine needles; catalog)

Web of Thread, 3240 Lone Oak Road, Suite 124, Paducah, KY, 42003 USA (unusual threads, "large eye" needles; catalog)

Resources

Full Spectrum Lighting: available in bulbs and 4' fluorescent tubes. Use only approved full spectrum lights; check health or lighting specialists for brands and ordering.

Fiberglass Teflon® Pressing Sheet: available from Valerie Hearder, P.O. Box 24 Mahone Bay, Nova Scotia, Canada, B0J 2E0.

Green Quilts: contact Susan Shie, 342 S. Walnut Street, Wooster, OH, 44691 USA (enclose three dollars for sample newsletter)

Stamps: contact Rubberstampmadness (RSM Enterprises), 408 SW Monroe #210, Corvallis, OR, 97333 USA (newsletter provides information on ordering from a variety of catalogs)

Footnotes

1. quoted in *Simpson's Contemporary Quotations* compiled by James B. Simpson. (Boston: Houghton Mifflin, 1988)
2. quoted in *The Art Quilt* by Penny McMorris and Michael Kile (Gualala, CA: The Quilt Digest Press, 1986). Used by permission.
3. Daly, *Beyond God the Father* (Boston: Beacon Press, 1973). Used by permission.
4. quoted in *Freeing the Creative Spirit* by Adriana Diaz (San Francisco: HarperSanFrancisco, a division of HarperCollins, 1992)
5. John Muir Papers, Holt-Atherton Dept. of Special Collections, University of the Pacific Libraries. ©1984 Muir-Hanna Trust. Used by permission.
6. Graham and DeMille, *Dance to the Piper* (Boston: Little Brown & Company, 1951)
7. Edwards, *Drawing on the Artist Within* (New York: Simon & Schuster, Inc., 1986) Copyright ©1986 by Betty Edwards. Reprinted by permisssion of Simon & Schuster, Inc.
8. Franck, *The Zen of Seeing* (New York: Vintage Books Edition/Random House, 1973)
9., 10., 13., 15., 16. quoted in *The Artist's Way: A Spiritual Path to Higher Creativity* by Julia Cameron (New York: Tarcher/Putnam, 1992) Quote from Miles Davis reproduced by permission, estate of Miles Davis.
11., 17. Henri, *The Art Spirit* (New York: Harper-Collins Publishers, Inc., 1984) Copyright 1923 J.B. Lippincott Company. Copyright renewed 1951 by Violet Organ. Introduction copyright 1930 by J.B. Lippincott Company. Copyright renewed 1958 by Forbes Watson. Reprinted by permission of HarperCollins Publishers, Inc.
12. Laury, *The Creative Woman's Getting It All Together at Home Handbook* (Fresno, CA: Hot Fudge Press, 1985) Published originally in 1977 by Van Nostrand Reinhold Company.
14. Nevelson, *Dawn and Dusks: Conversations with Diana McKown* (New York: Scribner & Sons, 1976) Used by permission.

Bibliography

Edwards, Betty. *Drawing on the Right Side of the Brain.* New York: Simon and Schuster, 1979

Godderis, Pam. *Ideas for Inspiration.* Alberta, Canada: Self-published, 1981

Swim, Laurie. *Quilting.* New York: Michael Friedman Publishing Group, Inc., 1993

For more information write for a free catalog from C&T Publishing
P.O. Box 1456
Lafayette, CA 94549
(1-800-284-1114)

About the Author

Valerie Hearder was born in the tropical city of Durban, South Africa. Its vibrant cultures and scenery laid the foundation for her use of color and the landscape form. The exotic city markets, abundant with African indigo cotton and Asian silks, fostered her passion for fabric. Valerie is a self-taught quilter and fabric artist.

Valerie left South Africa in 1975 to live in Yellowknife, Canada, just below the Arctic Circle. She later lived in Labrador for five years where she worked with the Inuit, Innu, and Settlers in the development of traditional crafts.

Valerie now lives with her husband and two children in Mahone Bay, Nova Scotia. For the past 11 years Valerie has taught and lectured in North America, South Africa, and Germany. Her work is held in both private and corporate collections and has appeared in numerous books and magazines including Nihon Vogue's *88 Leaders in the Quilt World Today*. She has written articles for quilting magazines in the United States, Canada, and Japan. *Beyond the Horizon* is her first book. Valerie enjoys hearing from quilters. She can be reached at Box 24 Mahone Bay, Nova Scotia, Canada, B0J 2E0.